EMBROIDERY
IN
FASHION

Embroidery in Fashion

ANNWEN NICHOLAS
and
DAPHNE TEAGUE

Pitman Publishing

First published 1975

SIR ISAAC PITMAN AND SONS LTD
Pitman House, 39 Parker Street, London WC2B 5PB, UK

PITMAN MEDICAL PUBLISHING CO LTD
42 Camden Road, Tunbridge Wells, Kent TN1 2QD, UK

FOCAL PRESS LTD
31 Fitzroy Square, London W1P 6BH, UK

PITMAN PUBLISHING CORPORATION
6 East 43 Street, New York, NY 10017, USA

FEARON PUBLISHERS INC
6 Davis Drive, Belmont, California 94002, USA

PITMAN PUBLISHING PTY LTD
Pitman House, 158 Bouverie Street, Carlton, Victoria, 3053,
Australia

PITMAN PUBLISHING
COPP CLARK PUBLISHING
517 Wellington Street West, Toronto M5V 1G1, Canada

SIR ISAAC PITMAN AND SONS LTD
Banda Street, PO Box 46038, Nairobi, Kenya

PITMAN PUBLISHING CO SA (PTY) LTD
Craighall Mews, Jan Smuts Avenue, Craighall Park,
Johannesburg 2001, South Africa

© Annwen Nicholas and Daphne Teague 1975

ISBN: 0 273 00018 7

Filmset and printed in Great Britain by
BAS Printers Limited, Wallop, Hampshire
Colour printing by Harrison & Sons (Hayes) Limited

G6007: 16

Preface

There have been many books published which have described and illustrated how one may find inspiration for, and understand what is meant by, embroidery, both in the specialist and general senses.

Only a comparatively small number of recent books touch on the various aspects of dress embroidery. There is therefore a limited field of bibliography from which to abstract information about contemporary dress embroidery.

It is the intention of this book to help fill this considerable gap and to concentrate on and emphasize the importance of fabrics and technique as the source of inspiration for dress embroidery.

Contents

Illustrations

Colour Plates

Acknowledgements

Manchester Polytechnic Faculty of Art and Design, Textile/Fashion Department

Cardiff College of Art

Stafford College of Further Education

Glamorgan Summer School

We are especially grateful to Keith Nicholas for co-ordinating and editing the script and manuscript;

to Bob Bissel and Ken Taylor who, between them, took most of the photographs;

and to Audrey Hunter for typing the manuscript.

Introduction

The term 'dress embroidery' has become inseparable from, and indeed almost synonymous with, 'fashion'. Thus the object of this book is not to relate directly to any set styles or patterns by illustrating various garments but to show the possibilities of fabrics and encourage originality and inventiveness in the methods of embroidery. By eradicating our preconceived ideas about the nature of dress embroidery we become more receptive to new fabrics and ideas and more creative in the use of traditional techniques.

To further these aims all aspects of dress embroidery will be incorporated, especially the adoption of traditional methods in the production of creative designs and the exploration of the general principles of design. In the latter, of great importance to dress embroidery is the close integration of the embroidery with the dress design, allowing for such functional considerations as the type of fabric to be used, the figure to be fitted and the occasions when the garment will be worn.

1 Historical Background

Adornment or added decoration has been one of man's instinctive expressions throughout the ages, whether it be of the body, personal belongings or dress. Dress embroidery has its beginnings in the sewing together of animal skins and the very early woven cloths, as is evident in primitive cave and later tomb paintings.

The limitations of materials on methods of embroidery have been basically similar until comparatively recent times. The early leather thong stitchery gave way to cotton

Fig. 1 Raised beadwork over string

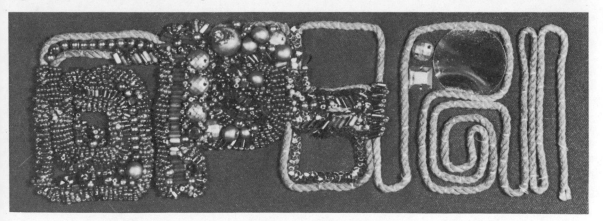

and silk embroidery indicative of man's technical progress. Many cultures have passed on their experience of embroidery down the ages with comparatively little variation, as a result of the limited availability of materials and implements.

Since mediaeval times decoration has been added to dress by means of stitchery. At various times in our history extensive decoration of dress has been fashionable and even the most sumptuous brocades and patterned fabrics were often further enriched by the addition of jewels, beads and decorative threads. Even these fabrics were produced from the same basic materials using technology which had been available from very early times.

Today we are inundated with an ever-expanding range of materials and fibres; there are at present well over 3000 man-made fabrics available but very few are household names. There are seven major groups into which these materials can be divided: cellulosics; polyamides (nylon); polyester (Terylene); acrylics; hydro-carbons; glass and polyurethanes. These numbers are bound to increase annually and add interesting 'unknown properties' to the range of materials available for adornment and embroidery.

This development accentuates the need for abandoning preconceived ideas and encouraging self-expression and experimentation which can only lead on to personal

Fig. 2 Polythene medallions with braid on hessian

discovery of what dress embroidery is and of what it can become.

2 The Appreciation of Fabrics

All branches of art which involve the use of materials, whatever form these may take, obtain their inspiration from an understanding of the nature of the medium in which the artist works.

The fashion embroiderer develops her creativity from a deep affection for and appreciation of the nature of fabrics. Materials are comprehended by the receptive faculties of the artist which include, to a greater or lesser degree, all of the five

Fig. 3 Collar, using etched metal rectangles, padded gold hide, beads and sequins

senses. Tactual and visual relationships with materials are most important, the handling and inspecting of different fabrics give intimate knowledge and means of recognition of each fabric's character and potential.

Research into fabrics is essential and a collection of the great variety available should be made, from the cheapest cotton to the most expensive embossed or watered silk. If a collection is to be made, fabrics could be arranged in the following categories:

  even to novelty
  dull to shiny
  rough to smooth
  thick to thin
  tough to fragile
  opaque to transparent

As this collection grows it will become obvious that these ranges of quality do not refer to one particular kind of material.

The easily recognizable properties of materials are all that have been discussed so far. Materials have other properties which are not so obvious and it is a knowledge of these latent properties which will ultimately determine their suitability to various categories of use, summed up as: working clothes; bedwear; children's wear; waterproofs; evening wear; playwear.

The word 'property' in the context of fabrics is defined as 'a quality or attribute common to the whole range of fabrics which is not necessary to distinguish each fabric from the other'. To illustrate what is meant by this, non-fraying fabrics can include materials ranging from felt and leather to

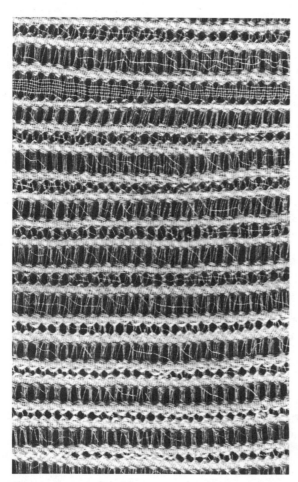

Fig. 4 Drawn thread

Fig. 5 Border pattern using layered organdie

4

bonded fabrics, all very different in appearance and to the touch but having the collective term 'non-fraying' attributed to them.

For the purpose of this book the apparent and latent properties and characteristics of groups of fabrics are discussed generally and illustrated to show how inspiration has developed from the knowledge of these distinguishing qualities.

Evenly woven fabrics

Fabrics such as cotton, linen and hessian are evenly woven. The warp and weft are equal and visually make a strong vertical and horizontal pattern. This even 'network' lends itself to any of the counted thread methods such as pattern darning, blackwork, pulled thread work and hardanger work. None of these methods introduces any alien element into the embroidery. The decoration that is added merely emphasizes the structure of the fabrics, all of which have easily separable threads, an essential property for these kinds of embroidery.

These techniques sound laborious and repetitive, with a total lack of spontaneity, but very interesting effects can be achieved by means of mixing two or more of these methods, as shown in the illustrations.

Transparent fabrics

Materials which can be enumerated in this class include: organdie, organza, net, voile, Terylene lawn, chiffon, nylon and polythene.

The 'see-through' quality of these fabrics makes possible endless variations by means of multiple layering of one or more of the materials, and interesting interplays and toning of colours can be achieved. An example of the darkening of colours using organdie is illustrated in Fig. 5. Colour plate 2 shows an example where the curling property of organdie is utilized to make an all-over pattern of curls, the automatic sewing machine having been first used for carrying out the embroidered pattern. The

shapes are cut as closely to the stitching as possible and the natural curl formed by winding the organdie around a pencil.

Stitching on both sides of these fabrics will naturally be visible and should be selected to suit the material, such as shadow work on organdie or muslin and darning stitches on net.

Surface-textured fabrics

Bouclé, corduroy (see Fig. 6), embossed cotton, fur fabric (see Fig. 7), lace, needle-cord, novelty weaves, piqué, robia voile, satin, velvets and velveteens all come under this heading and range from very heavily textured surfaces to smooth.

The treatments which can be applied to these textured fabrics are numerous and depend on an analysis of what the different qualities have to offer. Corduroy has a ribbing or furrowing which can be exploited with machine embroidery. A similar treatment could be given to fur fabric.

At the smooth end of the texture 'spectrum' satin, which can be made of silk or rayon, lends itself to quilting because of its

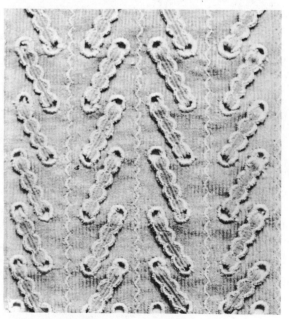

Fig. 6 Laced eyelets on corduroy

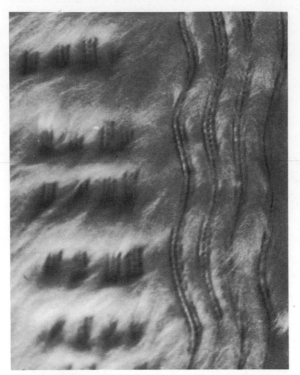

Fig. 7 Double needle stitching on fur fabric

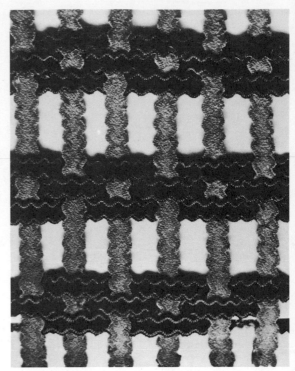

Fig. 9 Woven leather with automatic-machine pattern

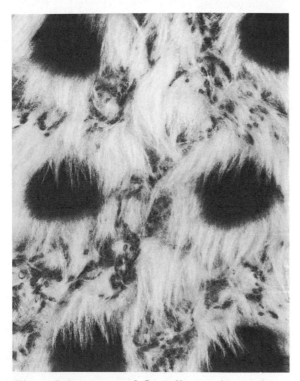

Fig. 8 Inlay spot and Cornelly mossing on fur fabric

sheen which reacts well to the fall of light on its surface, creating tonal changes.

Non-fraying fabrics

Bonded materials, felt, leather, paper cloth, suèdes, chamois and PVC are materials which can be classed as non-fraying. They are smooth and usually dense in construction with the exception of some bonded materials. Their greatest attribute is that they do not necessitate edge neatening and therefore have unlimited potential in experimental work using such techniques as punching, rolling, slotting, strip weaving and strap work.

Patterned fabrics

These can be both woven and printed and come in chevrons, checks, stripes, spots, diagonal twills, watered silk, brocaded satin and velvet.

Fig. 10 Figured velvet embroidered with feathers, beads and paillettes

All of these patterns can be used either by folding, tucking or pleating, using the basic print or woven pattern to dictate the treatment each is given. An evenly distributed design can thus be broken down to create a different pattern to which surface stitching may be added. Prints and woven patterns can be emphasized by machine embroidery, beads and hand stitches. The patterns can be completely covered giving an added dimension such as a glazed effect with sequins. Particular motifs may be highlighted but care has to be taken to avoid isolating the motifs which then fail to be read well from a distance.

Fig. 11 Tambour beading on printed voile

7

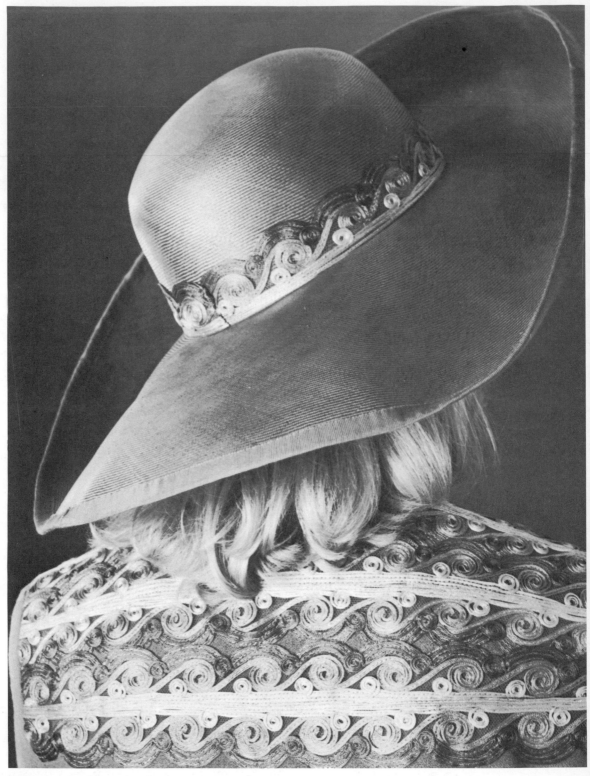

Fig. 12 Ribbon-braided yoke

3 Design in Relation to Fashion

The boundless design opportunities presented by the incredible ranges of materials must be rationalized relative to fashion. The following design considerations apply:

1 The decoration should enhance both the cut and appearance of the garment
The embroidery must be an integral part of the garment to enhance both the wear and the cut of the dress. The embroidery and garment should interact in the development of the garment as a whole, for instance an ornate embroidery may make it necessary to

have a simply cut garment.

Certain types of design are not suitable for some particular pattern shapes. An example of this can be seen when using a design based on straight lines and geometric shapes on a two-piece flared skirt: this problem could be overcome by using a six- or eight-gored skirt pattern (see Fig. 13A and B).

2 The decoration should not be isolated
The decoration must not be separated from the cut and appearance of a garment, if one

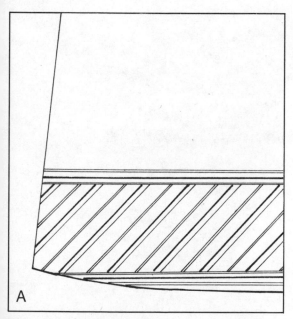

Fig. 13A Two-piece skirt showing distortion of design on the hemline

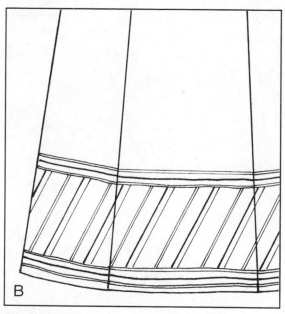

Fig. 13B A gored skirt showing possible solution

9

supersedes the other the whole effect will be one of imbalance.

3 A garment ought only to have a simple theme or one predominant area of interest
The result of contravening this basic precept is a loss of unity and emphasis. A typical example would be the use of scattered motifs or areas of embroidery on various parts of the garment, whereas a judiciously situated concentration of embroidery forming one focal point generally achieves a unifying effect.

4 Suitability of design and technique to their purpose
It must be remembered that a garment must fit a three-dimensional form, and that the cutting of a flat piece of material and the use of seams and darts to effect a fit will impose limitations on the type of embroidery. A good example of this is quilting when, if squares or diamonds are used, the fitting lines will distort any vertical or horizontal lines. This limitation can be overcome by working out the design lines on the pattern pieces or on a dress stand by means of tape or wool, prior to making up.

5 Suitability of cloth to design
This is an obvious requirement; however in practice it is more difficult to assess and indeed this may only be done by trial and error until experience of different materials gives one a basis upon which to work.

An example of the wrong use of cloth would be an attempt to closely smock a felt dress.

Fig. 14A Facecloth jacket front

Fig. 14B Facecloth jacket sleeve

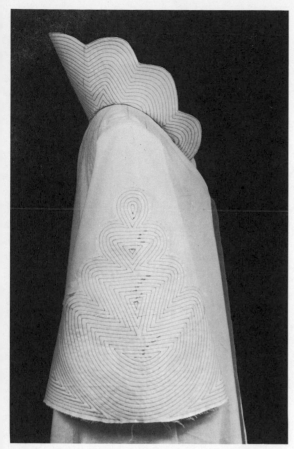

Fig. 15 Positioning of the embroidery on the toile

6 Relationship of the embroidery to the figure and the form of the garment

Great care must be taken to ensure that any embroidery used is considered in relation to the figure of the wearer and the form of the garment. A preliminary and essential step in assessing this relationship is effected by preparing a 'mock-up' or toile. The toile can be made up in a cheaper material such as mull or calico, having properties and weight similar to the fabric which it is proposed finally to use. The toile can then be used to work out the fit of the garment and the positioning of the embroidery (see Fig. 15).

The latter can be executed by pencil marking the toile or by the application of another material to achieve a massed appearance. An all-round visual assessment can now be made and this is done paying special attention to the weight of the embroidery in relation to the garment and the figure for which it is intended.

7 The effects of embroidery situation and body movement

The positioning of the embroidery must be functionally related to bodily movement, for example friction can result from arm movement when beading and highly textured embroidery is located on both bodice and sleeves.

8 Will the finished embroidered garment fulfil the functional demands made on it?

The properties of the embroidery materials should be properly understood and related to their functional requirements.

Garments which require washing should be embroidered only with threads and techniques that accommodate washing. For example, easily laundered background fabric can be embellished with machine embroidery.

Clothes for special occasions such as wedding or evening dresses can be more lavishly embroidered and the choice of effects can be more adventurous than for daywear.

9 Is the weight of the cloth suitable for embellishment?

Not all fabrics are sufficiently strong to take the weight of embroidery without drag occurring, but cloth can be backed to eliminate this defect. However, should the material be light and flowing, like chiffon, its inherent value would be lost if such precautions were taken. It is for this reason that an appropriate embroidery technique must be used, such as light machine embroidery, hand shadow work and their variations.

10 Will the amount of drag on the cloth, resulting from the embellishment, impede the fit of the garment?

Excessive weight of embroidery can sometimes cause drag and result in a badly fitting garment. This is often the case where only one part of the article is embroidered. An example would be heavy embroidery to the front of a garment weighing down and dragging it off balance, thus causing great discomfort to the wearer and distortion of the fabric.

11 Is the decorative quality of the chosen fabric sufficient without embellishment?

The colour and texture of a cloth are attributes which can be satisfying without embellishment. Of the two, colour has more to offer the eye as there are more variations available. Texture is only visible by virtue of the surface variations of light and shade.

Fancy weaves, such as basket effects or simple twill, can set up a visual tension or relationship, especially if taken advantage of in the cut of the garment, which could in itself be satisfactory. Embroidery has to be complementary and robust in character to combat this and become related to the entire garment.

12 Does the method of embroidery grow out of, enhance, or is it imposed on, the fabric?

Traditional openwork techniques such as drawn thread, pulled fabric and needle weaving enrich and adjust the basic fabric by producing openwork structures. The cloth is thereby given a more sparse but enhanced appearance which both maintains and develops from the essential character of the fabric.

There are so many woven materials available that, providing a suitable fabric is selected for the type of embroidery chosen, practically any material can be utilized.

The natural qualities of hand-woven fabrics such as Indian silk, rough Indian cotton and linens make excellent bases for hand stitching where the threads and stitches merge into and enhance the background.

To *impose* a method of embroidery implies the addition of an alien or incongruous fabric as a form of decoration on an unrelated base. This pitfall awaits even the best-intentioned embroiderers and can only be avoided by experience.

Colour, tone and texture

There are three elements of prime importance which have to be considered in fashion and fashion embroidery; these are colour, tone and texture. Everybody has some awareness of these qualities in clothing, though perhaps colour is best understood. The reason for this is that choice of colour for everyday garments is a personal thing with each individual's likes and dislikes being governed by emotions, personal prejudice (green is unlucky!) and years of experience of the colours which suit them best.

The average person is not particularly aware of tone and texture other than that tone is vaguely something to do with colour and texture is to do with the feel of a material. All of which means that, generally speaking, the fashion sense of the average individual is a combination of instinct and sensibilities. Both of these must be part of the embroiderer's make-up, but it is the understanding of colour, tone and texture of materials which integrates the fashion embroiderer's art. It is the intention of this chapter to establish a basis upon which such an understanding can be built.

Colour, tone and texture are inherent in any piece of fashion embroidery and whilst all three can be seen, texture alone can be felt. Texture, however, does produce tonal effects on colour and hence neither colour, tone nor texture can be discussed in the context of material without reference to at least one of the others.

Fashion and fashion embroidery have a great advantage over most other forms of art because the fabrics and materials used provide colour from the commencement of the work. All the effects which are obtainable from natural or synthetic threads and fabrics

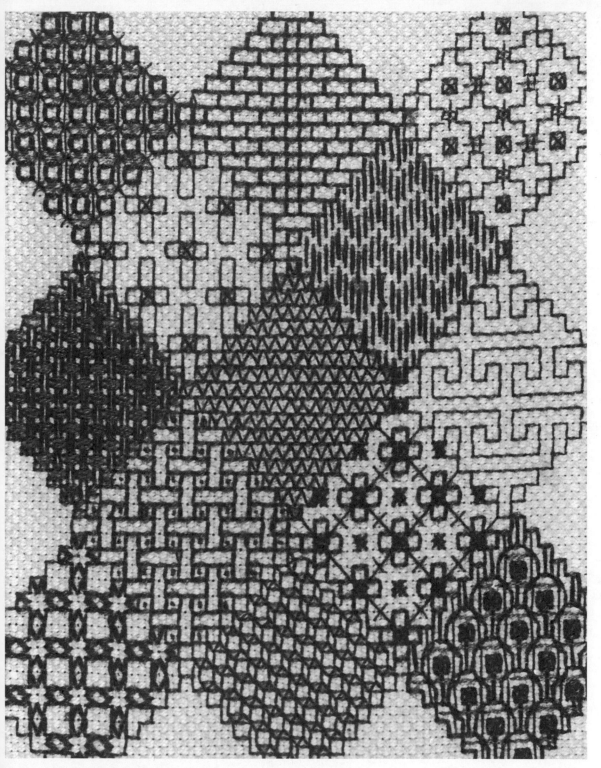

*Fig. 16 Blackwork sample illustrating tonal
variations caused by stitch patterns*

are a result of the different surface characteristics embodied in the materials.

Tone produced by texture is caused by varying amounts of light or shadow falling on a surface and being reflected by it. The degree of tonal strength of a fabric increases from light to dark depending on the robustness of the texture and its ability to create shadow. The simple rule which follows from this is: the smoother the texture the lighter the tone; the heavier the texture the darker the tone.

This rule is true for all colours of materials, but of course if the colour of the material is dark then the tonal effect of texture is reduced unless the material happens to be very shiny. A shiny material is subject to the same tonal rules as other textured materials but it will have this extra 'sparkle' characteristic which will accentuate its texture even if it is black in colour.

It is essential to understand the tonal properties of materials and in order to discover them for oneself the following experiments should be carried out.

Combine the following contrasting materials:

1 opaque fabrics with transparent fabrics;
2 matt materials with shiny materials;
3 heavily textured fabrics with slightly textured fabrics.

Carrying out various permutations of these will give valuable insight into their possibilities.

Discover other methods of achieving tonal effects by investigating samples of:

1 padding
2 drawn fabric
3 drawn thread
4 needle weaving
5 blackwork
6 stitch direction
7 stitch texture

Having established a simple rule of texture's tonal effect on colour, an understanding of colour relationships is necessary.

It is not intended to expand a great deal on the theory of colour, about which there are several standard works. However, some

Fig. 17 Black, shiny and matt fabrics, Trapunto quilted and beaded, illustrating tonal variations

of the basic terms should be understood and the following selection gives quite a broad coverage.

Colour circle: a selection of spectrum colours arranged in a circle. There are different arrangements of the spectrum colours to be found and these relate to the differing theories expounded in the standard works of such people as Itten, Ostwald and Munsell.

Hue: a term which defines the basic spectrum colour.

Chroma: the strength of a colour decreasing from maximum hue strength to neutral grey.

Value: the amount of black or white in a colour.

Tint: a tint is made by adding white to a hue, e.g. light blue.

Shade: a shade is made by adding black to a hue, e.g. dark orange (i.e. brown).

Harmonic colours: a range of colours closely

related in the spectrum, e.g. red–orange, blue–turquoise.

Complementary colours: colours opposite each other on the colour circle, e.g. orange – green, blue – yellow.

Discords: colours in a relationship where their basic contrasting hue strengths have been upset. An example of this is brown set against lilac, brown being a shade of orange and lilac being a tint of purple. Purple is normally darker than orange. The over-turning of the natural relationship tends to agitate the eye.

After-image: if a colour such as yellow is stared at for a period of time and then the eyes are closed an image of complementary colouring, which in this case would be blue/purple, is briefly retained on the retina.

Colour impinges on the eye and varying arrangements of colour produce different reactions. Careful consideration must be given to these effects as the success or failure of a design may depend on it.

Harmonies of colours have natural relationships which can be readily understood but, if over used, may prove to be monotonous. The addition of a contrast of hue or a subtle discord may overcome this hazard.

Complementary colours have mutually complementary after-images and tend to appeal to the eye for this reason.

Discords and tonal contrast tend to excite the eye and add interest. Intensive use of discords can create a disturbing effect upon the eye which may or may not be intended.

It is through a knowledge of these characteristic visual reactions to colour that differing moods and effects are achieved.

Tonal interaction of one hue upon another is a fascinating property of colour and, if applied to materials, is one of the most exciting facets of fashion. If one piece of fabric, which in itself is of satisfactory colour and design, has another coloured material added to it, it changes tonally relative to the added material, depending upon its colour and size (see colour plate 4A and B). The addition of yet another coloured element would bring about another change in the apparent colour and tone of the two original materials. The effects thus obtainable are infinite and, proceeding with this line of thought to its logical conclusion, the same garment will change in appearance on a different wearer depending on that person's shape and colouring of the hair, skin and eyes.

Colour, tone and texture in a garment can make a figure appear larger or smaller than it actually is. For example, light, bright and shiny fabrics and embroidery materials such as beads, sequins, Lurex and metallic threads, all tend to give an impression of increased size while darker matt tones give a slimming effect. Ill-considered permutations of colour, tone and texture can result in unfortunate effects and illusions of shape on the figure of the wearer. Pattern and line applied to a garment can also have the same poor results if no account is taken of the effects which will be produced.

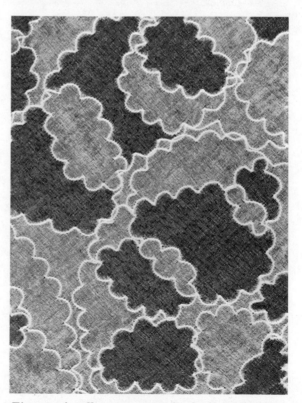

Fig. 18 An all-over pattern in single and double-layered organdie

Fig. 19 Chequered organdie with beads

Fig. 20 Cross-stitch pattern

The earlier reference to harmonies producing a monotonous effect can also apply to an arrangement of several differing colours all having been reduced to the same tone. (It is interesting to note that equally toned colours come within Ostwald's definition of a harmony.) This monotony can only be avoided by varying tone. A monochromatic embroidery can be made exciting by means of strongly contrasting tones. Varying tones of black and white can be particularly attractive and the use of layered transparent fabric (see Figs 18 and 19) can give strong and very interesting tonal effects.

It has already been established that tonal effects are created on coloured fabrics by means of the variations of texture, and that texture is a tactually discernible surface quality.

The texture or surface quality of a material must not be confused with surface pattern which will be found, for example, on a printed textile. Although surface pattern may provide tonal relationships and a superficial appearance of texture, no variations will be apparent to the touch.

Texture may be random, as for example a cluster of beads sewn together, or it may be ordered (see Fig. 20), having a definite arrangement or pattern; the same beads may be sewn on at regular intervals.

Practically any one material can be applied to another to provide texture but, in dress embroidery, the effect of the applied texture is of paramount importance to the wearability of the garment. Even if the embroidery has excellent qualities when viewed subjectively, it cannot be judged successful if it makes the garment impractical.

4 Preparation of an Embroidered Garment

It is important to understand the theory upon which the preparation method for an embroidered garment is based. The principles are quite simple and logical and relate to the need for stability of the individual pattern pieces which go to make up any garment.

A garment which is simply made up from non-embellished material has pattern pieces which are already 'stabilized', that is they are not subjected to change, and, provided that it is well made, the garment will fit the wearer with no distortion to mar its appearance. The addition of embroidery to this fitted garment will result in several possible defects, such as wrinkling, pulling, sagging and effective shrinking. It is to avoid these that embroidery is added to individual pattern pieces, under tension if possible, and precautions like damp stretching are taken prior to making up. Herein lies the difference between the making up of an embroidered garment and that of a straightforward plain one.

Experience shows that small pieces of embroidered fabric are prone to fraying and difficult to handle, possibly producing poor results. For economy of effort and ease of

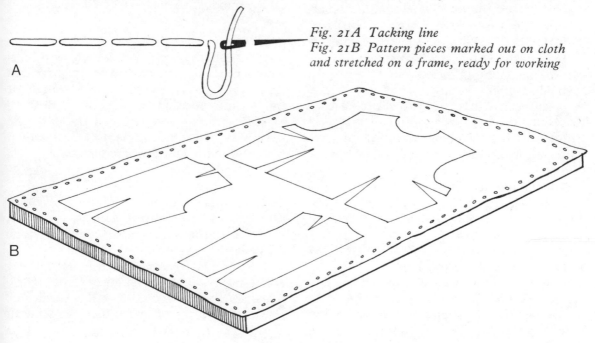

Fig. 21A Tacking line
Fig. 21B Pattern pieces marked out on cloth and stretched on a frame, ready for working

A

B

17

handling it is advisable to mark out several pattern pieces on one manageable piece of cloth.

Many types of embroidery, both hand and machine, need to have the fabric stretched on a frame for working. This discourages distortion and wrinkling but necessitates extra allowances around pattern pieces. Besides this, extra seam allowances are needed between each pattern piece because shrinkage can result from adding embroidery to a fabric. A 102 mm/4-in. allowance should be left between each pattern piece so that pattern pieces can be extended if necessary.

The large tolerances which these recommendations imply call for considerable wastage of material so that the quantities of fabric and form of layout, as suggested on commercial pattern literature in particular, must be recalculated and adjusted accordingly.

It is important that the method chosen for marking out the pattern pieces and embroidered areas on a garment has a semi-permanent quality able to withstand the extra handling which the pattern pieces receive whilst being embroidered. The normal methods of marking have certain disadvantages; tailor's chalk and carbon marking are too easily brushed off and looped tailor tacks may become entangled in beads and stitchery during working. A continuous marking tack about 12 mm/½ in. long which picks up only one or two threads between each stitch is an excellent form of marking (see Fig. 21A). This will clearly define not only the actual seam line but any darts, pleats and tucks or any other feature of the garment.

On completing the marking out of the pattern pieces it is now necessary to mark out the embroidery design. This can be done in a number of ways:

1 Tacked tracing or tissue paper
The design should be drawn with a fine line on to tracing or tissue paper and then secured in the correct position on to the fabric pattern pieces. The design lines are transferred by sewing through both the paper and cloth using small running stitches, and the paper is removed carefully on completion. If the design is complex and a lot of tacking lines are necessary, which will prove difficult to remove amongst the embroidery, it is preferable to use threads which nearly match the ground fabric. Marking lines of this nature should never be tugged out in lengths but cut individually and removed with tweezers if necessary.

2 Prick and pounce
The design should be drawn out on to a strong tracing paper then, using a needle or special pricker, a series of holes is pierced along the design lines. The fabric is pinned out on to a firm surface or stretched on a frame with the design pinned in position. The pounce powder is dabbed on to the tracing paper with a soft pad and gently rubbed over the surface so that the powder is forced through the holes. At this stage it is only a semi-permanent form of marking but it can be made permanent by going over the dots with a white water-colour or gouache paint using a fine brush. This method is very useful where repetitive motifs are required.

3 Templates
This is another method which is useful where repetitive shapes make up a design. The thick paper templates are tacked or pinned into position on the fabric and small tacking stitches are worked around the periphery of each. The templates are then removed and re-used where necessary.

4 Transparent fabrics
Transferring designs on to transparent or semi-transparent fabrics such as organdie, organza, crêpe and chiffon can be done fairly easily.

The design is drawn on tracing or cartridge paper and placed under the fabric which has been secured to a flat surface or frame. The design lines are then drawn with a fine paint line on the right side of the fabric. Fine running-tack lines through the fabric only can be an alternative method of marking, as damp stretching could cause the paint line to bleed. Paint of a colour close to that of the fabric is therefore essential.

The design, having been transferred to the pattern pieces, may now be worked in embroidery. It is advisable to complete as much of the embroidery as possible before removing from the frame, damp stretching (where necessary) and cutting out the individual pattern pieces prior to making up the garment.

Small areas around the darts, faced edges and seam lines must be left free of embroidery to allow for easy machining when making up the garment. Gaps formed in this way can be embroidered over after darts, facings and seams have been sewn. This is particularly necessary when using beads and sequins or very bulky threads, as the machine presser foot must clear any obstructions, otherwise broken needles and an erratic stitch line will result.

When filling in these spaces over seams and darts with embroidery great care must be taken to ensure that the tensions of the added work are not too great, otherwise distortion along these infill areas may spoil the garment.

Order of work
1 Stretch fabric out on to a flat surface or frame (depending on size and number of pattern pieces).
2 Arrange lay.
3 Tack out pattern pieces.
4 Mark out area to be embroidered.
5 Cut marked cloth into large manageable pieces to be embroidered, preferably rectangular, and stretch if required.
6 Embroider as method suggests, leaving darts and pattern piece edges free of embroidery; this is usually for all-over patterns or for linking motifs on side seams or where necessary. Check pattern pieces for size.
7 Remove work from frame, damp stretch if required and check pattern piece sizes.
8 Sew up darts and side seams and fill in gaps, matching motifs or pattern texture and shape, and complete the garment.

Darts and seams can be pressed by ironing on the wrong side of the garment using a thick, soft pad underneath.

5 Technical Hints

Frames

The use of an embroidery frame and the time involved in its preparation and use are regarded by many as something with which only professionals bother. This attitude is wrong and the amateur is bound to agree once the results of using a frame are seen and the convenience which it affords is experienced.

A frame gives ease and comfort in working, safeguards against puckering and distortion and also helps towards achieving regular stitches which are particularly necessary for hand quilting.

There are two types of frames: the simple tambour hoop or ring used for machine embroidery and small motifs, and a slate frame which is more generally used for hand work.

DRESSING A FRAME

The advantage of using a slate frame or stretcher (as a substitute) is that all thicknesses of fabric can be stretched successfully for working on.

1　Starting at the centre of each roller and working to the right and then left, with overcast stitch sew the fabric or backing fabric to the webbing which is attached to both rollers.

2　By pegging the slats into position the material is made tight. If the backing and fabric is too long for the slats it can be rolled on to the rollers and unwound as required.

3　The remaining sides of the fabric are now fixed to the slats with string which is laced through the fabric and over the wooden slats and thus tightened until drum-like.

4　If a backing fabric is necessary the pattern pieces are now sewn on to the dressed frame using long-and-short stitch. Make certain that grains of both fabrics are straight.

USE OF A STRETCHER OR PICTURE FRAME

If the fabric is too large for a slate frame and it is necessary to obviate the damage which the rolling up of worked and surplus fabric may cause, the use of an old simple picture frame or canvas stretcher is recommended. It is also a quicker method and often more convenient for working on odd pattern pieces than a slate frame. The woodwork-minded embroiderer can easily construct one by making use of 50 mm × 25 mm/ 2-in. × 1-in. wood, jointed by means of half housing joints or by using metal corrugated fasteners.

As with a slate frame, material can be attached to a picture frame with or without a backing fabric.

The fabric to be embroidered is stretched on the straight of grain on to a frame and secured by either gold-headed pins or staples. If a backing fabric is needed it is put on the frame first in the manner indicated, then the material to be embroidered is stretched over the frame in a similar way, pinned on as shown in Fig. 25 or sewn on as in the slate frame method.

In some instances, when a delicate fabric

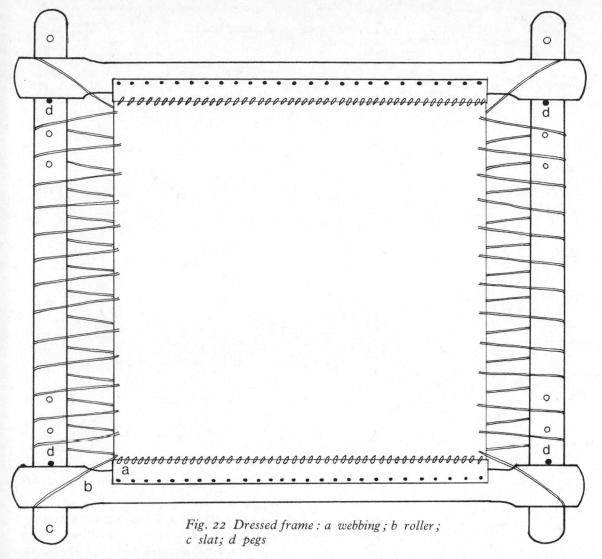

Fig. 22 *Dressed frame : a webbing; b roller; c slat; d pegs*

like chiffon or net is stretched in this way, added strength is needed where tension from pinning arises but it is possible that the effect would be spoiled if the work were to be backed. This problem can be overcome by stretching the backing and fabric on the frame and attaching them both together by a sewn line as close to the edge as possible. The backing fabric is cut away carefully up to this line, leaving the pattern piece free of backing while being supported on the frame. This is also used with slate framing.

TO AVOID PUCKERING

Organdie, net, muslin or fine lawn can be

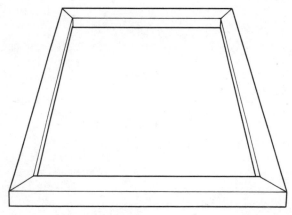

Fig. 23 *Wooden stretcher*

21

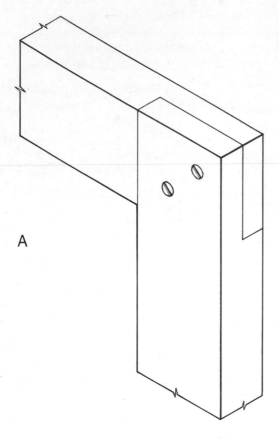

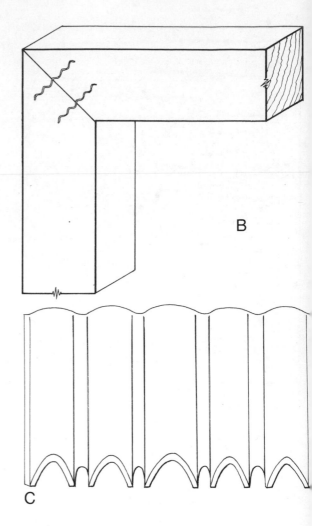

Fig. 24A Half housing joint
    B Joint with fastener
    C Metal corrugated fastener

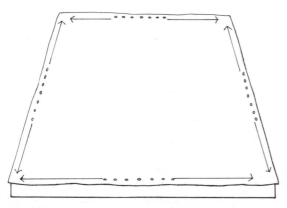

Fig. 25 Wooden stretcher with cloth attached

used as a backing to avoid puckering on such fine fabrics as crêpe-de-chine and satin. The two are placed together and the embroidery worked as though they were one fabric. The superfluous backing fabric is then cut away up to the embroidery.

Damp stretching

The principle behind damp stretching is that puckered and distorted pieces can be shrunk and pulled back into shape easily if fibres are dampened and then left to dry. This almost takes the place of damp pressing which cannot easily be applied to a heavily textured surface. Most fabrics can be damp stretched, except those which watermark and those that tarnish. These susceptible

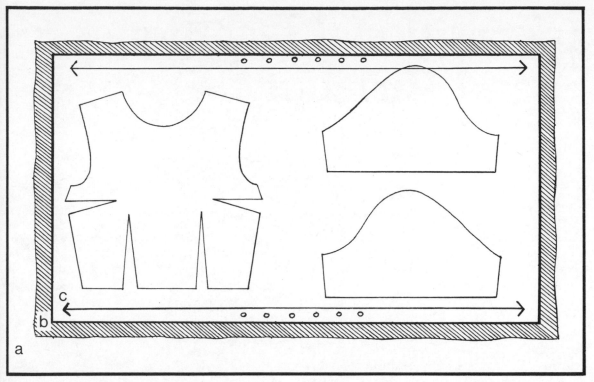

*Fig. 26 Damp stretching on a wooden surface :
a table top ; b damp sheet ; c embroidered
pieces*

fabrics ought to be embroidered on a slate frame and as a result they should be sufficiently stretched to eliminate any need for stretching on removal from the frame. Watermarking can be avoided by stretching the pieces on an almost dry cloth. It is advisable to check the manufacturer's recommendations on fabrics before damp stretching.

METHOD

1 Leave the embroidered pieces in large rectangular sections, never cut them up after initial completion. The bigger the sections to be stretched, the better and more easily handled they are.

2 A blanket (flannelette) or a clean, dye-fast cotton sheet is wetted and spun dry—this makes it sufficiently damp so as not to watermark the fabric but to allow the work to dampen evenly all over. This is placed on a flat wooden surface.

3 The embroidered pieces are laid on and pinned to the wooden surface through the blanket. Use large, non-rust drawing pins.

4 The order of pinning is important. Starting on the straightest edge, place the first pin at the centre point and work out to left and then right, placing pins at 12 mm/$\frac{1}{2}$-in. intervals. Pins must be placed on a straight grain line.

5 Directly opposite the first central pin, applying a little tension along the straight grain, place a pin. Continue in similar manner applying slight tension to the embroidery until all four sides are complete and the whole area flat. If there are any stubborn puckers or wrinkles and the fabric permits, water can be sprayed on to the area and dabbing pressure applied with the palm of the hand until the whole is flattened and shrunk. A garden spray is recommended.

6 Check that the paper pattern pieces still fit the now stretched embroidered pieces. Make adjustments by removing some pins and easing and pulling until shapes fit.

7 Remove the pins, cut out and make up the garment.

6 Traditional Techniques and Variations

All embroidery techniques are limited by and developed from the available materials, threads and colours. In the past certain limitations were imposed by the range of materials available, but overall results depended on the nimble fingers and patience of the embroiderers. The majority of these limitations have now disappeared with the introduction of vast numbers of new materials and coloured threads and a similar increase in the complexity and variety of tools.

Traditional methods thus present many opportunities for experiment by means of using the basic theory but with the new colours and materials now to hand. In the last chapter the properties of fabrics were discussed with reference to their use in designing. With the traditional techniques and design methods established, the choice of materials and design of garments are restricted to those which are appropriate to the method chosen. Invention thus grows out of the technique itself and the variety of colours and materials which can be made to conform to or translate the method.

Some of the traditional techniques which govern the type of design for a garment include faggoting, where strips of material are joined together, thus directly affecting its shape and line. In the same way patchwork (see Fig. 27), or the joining together of pieces of fabric to form a new fabric, will affect design no matter what new materials or colours are available.

The drawn thread technique demands the use of an evenly woven material regardless of what the material is made of, and so again the design of a garment stems directly from the nature of the weave and the possibilities of design within the technique.

Appliqué

Appliqué, as its name suggests, is the application of one fabric to another and as a method of embroidery it is the oldest, probably having been developed originally by the Persians and the Indians. The Greeks and Egyptians made lavish use of it and when the Crusades were fought in the Middle Ages the high ideals of the Christian knights were expressed in the rich appliqué work on their accoutrements, which included such items as horse trappings, surcoats and banners.

DESIGN
There are two forms of appliqué, these being inlay and onlay, and by far the most use is made of the latter. Inlay as a technique will be discussed towards the end of this chapter.

As appliqué is concerned with the application of one or more materials to another the relationships and properties of the fabrics thus united must be considered. Fortunately, almost all fabrics are suitable for use in this method of embroidery, even those with the widely differing characteristics typified in

*Fig. 27 Patchwork jacket showing the effect
of design on edge detail*

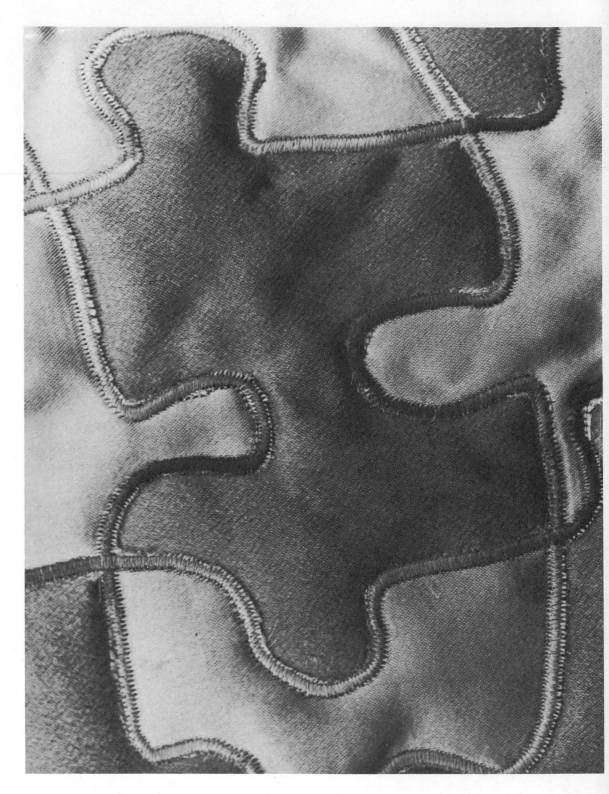

Fig. 28 Satin appliqué

such materials as heavy brocades and velvets, leather and felt, silk and satin, organdie and net. Even stretch fabric can be applied if it is suitably backed with a stiffening material like Vilene or an equivalent. An interesting variation is Piave embroidery which combines net and organdie, the organdie being cut away to reveal net areas beneath.

The main problem encountered in applying one material to another is the means by which the dividing line, that is the edge of the fabric to be applied, is treated. It may be desirable to emphasize the edges, in which case they may be rolled, outlined with couching, hemmed, cut, torn, hemstitched, frayed, fringed, machined with zig-zag stitches or applied to the background with decorative hand stitches of which button-hole, blanket and herringbone stitch are typical examples. This separation from the ground may not be the aim of the embroiderer and hard edges can be made to merge into the background by softening or hiding them with seeding stitches, beads, et cetera.

The outline or edge of an applied material encloses its shape and the character of the material determines the kind of shape which may be used. A firmly delineated edge should contain no sharp internal or external corners if the material is a woven fabric, as the sharp corners or points tend to disappear when hand or machine stitched into place. More suitable materials are available to provide a sharp pointed effect and these include suède, leather and felt which may particularly be used to advantage.

Applied shapes in dress embroidery can be used to highlight selected features such as pockets or cuffs; alternatively, whole areas of garments such as bodices or sleeves may be covered with selected shapes which can be arranged in patterns. The patterns may be straightforward repetitive ones or may vary through graduation of shape and size, thus eliminating what otherwise might be an uninteresting effect or even a cluttered one. The risk of creating a cluttered or bitty effect with appliqué in the context of fashion is diminished if the self-colour of

Fig. 29 Appliqué and quilted and beaded butterflies

the material is allowed to dominate and the embroidery is used to create tonal effects which grow out of the background fabric. This is not to say that colour variations are forbidden; a flamboyant occasion calls for an equally flamboyant dress which can have correspondingly excitingly coloured appliqué. Generally speaking however, subtlety in applied fabric colour produces more effective results.

The use of similarly coloured materials with contrasting textures, such as black velvet applied to black wool or organdie or suède applied to leather, can produce exciting effects and be most successful in dress embroidery (see Fig. 17). Additional hand or machine stitchery can be used to modulate or emphasize these contrasts with related or contrasting tonal and textural effects.

The richness and variety afforded by appliqué work make it one of the most creative of traditional techniques, but as a method of dress embroidery it is one of the more difficult methods to handle successfully

27

Fig. 30 Counterchange idea used for inlay of appliqué

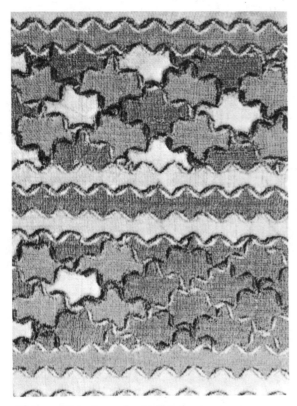
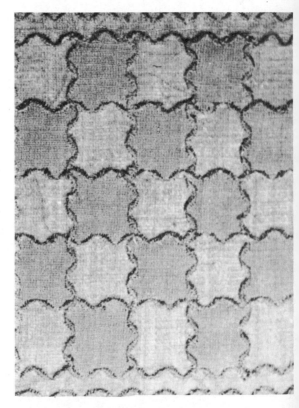

Fig. 31 Cut-through appliqué using an automatic pattern stitch as an outline

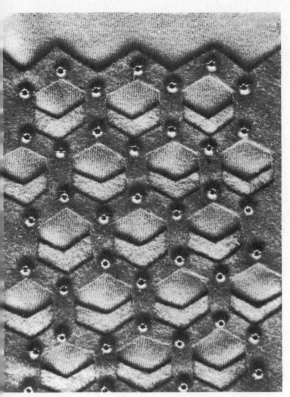

Fig. 32 Felt overlay

materials. Two layers of fabric are machined together in a selected design, the top layer is then cut away in selected areas to reveal the lower material. The machined pattern can be formed using two adjacent parallel lines of straight machine stitching or a machined satin stitch may be used to avoid possible fraying out.

Although further embellishment may not be felt necessary, it is possible to add enrichment to all types of appliqué work using embroidery stitches. Here again restraint is necessary as the effectiveness of the appliqué may be diminished, especially if it is inlay where an over-abundance of stitching could kill the expression of the method.

As with all methods of embroidery an understanding of the characteristics and limitations of the materials is essential. The chief factors which influence the application of one woven material to another are the warp and the weft of both the appliqué pieces and the background material (see Fig. 33A and B). These must correspond in direction otherwise wrinkling and pulling will result where they occur on the bias.

because it calls for a good deal of restraint by the embroiderer when faced with the wealth of available alternatives.

Inlay offers yet another alternative to the broad spectrum of effects obtainable in appliqué. It is a self-explanatory term and consists of the laying in of a piece of one material into an exactly similar shaped gap in another material.

This method is ideally suited for designs which involve counterchange. For maximum effect to be achieved absolute accuracy in the cutting of shapes is essential so that no gaps are present when one shape is laid into another. The meeting edges of the materials are joined by means of hemming or a decorative couched line worked immediately over the join. Felt, leather, suède and other non-fraying materials are suitable for this method of work.

There is a variation of inlay known as the 'cut through' method suitable for other

WORKING METHOD

1   The relationship of the appliqué pieces to the shape of the garment can be appreciated by means of arranging paper replica shapes on to a toile of the garment. In this way any scale alterations can be made before the actual materials are cut.

2   Check the way that the paper shapes relate to the warp and the weft of the toile and mark the straight of grain on the individual pieces.

3   Tack out the paper garment pattern pieces and arrange the paper motif pieces according to the straight of grain, locating them by means of tacking. Allow as much fabric around the pattern pieces as possible. This should be at least 76 mm/3 in. to allow for pinning on a frame for working and stretching when finished. This rule applies to all embroidery methods used for dress.

4   Cut out the motif pieces allowing for turnings if the method warrants it, and

29

A

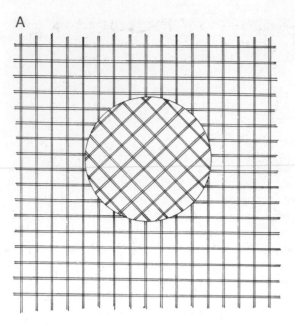

B

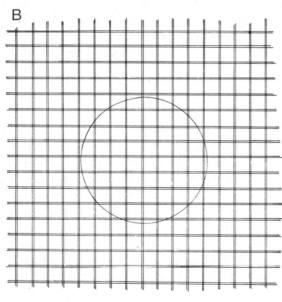

Fig. 33A Incorrect application of shape
Fig. 33B Correct application of shape with
grain corresponding to background fabric

arrange and tack on to the garment pattern pieces ready for machining or hand stitching.

This completes the preparation and the decoration can now be added if required. All work of an elaborate nature such as blind hemming and hemstitching needs to be worked on a slate frame, likewise further embellishment to appliqué with beads or handstitching must be worked in this way in order to avoid puckering. A large picture frame is a good substitute for a slate frame, the pattern pieces being pinned out on the frame with or without a backing and worked accordingly.

APPLIQUÉ AND SEWING OF LEATHER AND SUÈDE

Materials like leather and suède present the beginner with various problems. Position pinning or unpicking of sewing leaves permanent marks or perforations so that careful planning is necessary to avoid any such defects. Clear adhesive tape or fusible fleece can be used to fix the pieces in position when the process of arranging and sewing is under way. Other non-fraying fabrics can be dealt with in a similar manner. Any unwanted perforations in leather can be concealed by means of carefully filling the holes with Cow gum applied on the end of a pin.

Close satin stitch should be avoided when applying leather or plastic as the result is a 'postage stamp' effect with the applied patches being too easily torn from the backing.

These materials have a tendency to stick to the presser foot of sewing machines. This difficulty can be overcome by the use of a 'Teflon' foot if available; if not, a thin sheet of transparent paper can be used between the foot and the material, and it is also possible to follow a pattern drawn on this non-stick agent.

Leather can vary in thickness and any thin patches should be located and marked on the back and avoided when work is being carried out. Motif shapes may be marked out on the back of leather or plastic prior to cutting them. Any edge marking which might result from front marking can thus be avoided.

Fig. 34 (Above) Appliqué of leather and velvet on a woollen fabric

Fig. 35 (Below) Machine-quilted leather showing unwanted perforations

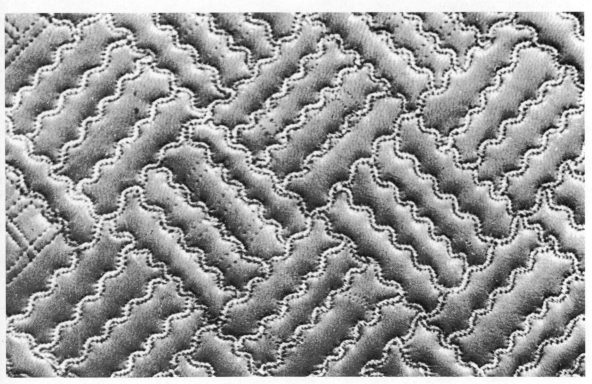

Bead and sequin embroidery

Bead and sequin embroidery is a fairly costly and time-consuming form of dress decoration. Despite this fact it is possibly the best liked of all the different varieties of embroidery techniques available. The reason for this is the quality of luxury and richness it imparts to the appearance of any garment.

Throughout history people have enriched their clothes by adding decoration, usually in the form of jewellery, beads and sequins. The reigns of Henry VIII and Elizabeth I illustrate this point aptly because it was a period when richly decorative fabrics were embellished further by the use of precious and semi-precious stones and pearls. To add to this feeling of extravagance many garments which were often made up of two or three different embroidered fabrics were accompanied by an array of encrusted jewellery.

The 1920s was a period when beads and sequin embroidery became popular, particularly for evening wear. The simple shift-shaped garment of this era provided the maximum uninterrupted area for an all-over pattern in beads, sequins and diamanté. These were often combined with Cornelly machine embroidery on fine crêpe-de-chine and georgette. So popular was this fashion that machine-stitched and tambour-beaded garments were bought ready to 'sew up'.

DESIGN

Bead embroidery involves the addition of 'material' which protrudes from and is alien to a fabric; it therefore follows that as a decoration it cannot form an integral part of the fabric. Its main use is to add interest to a plain surface or to emphasize a colour or form on a patterned fabric. It is therefore important that beads are used boldly and creatively to enrich a fabric rather than to complicate it. The finished result should give a thick encrusted effect making the most of the richness of texture, light and shade of both embroidery and fabric.

The intrinsic nature of bead embroidery

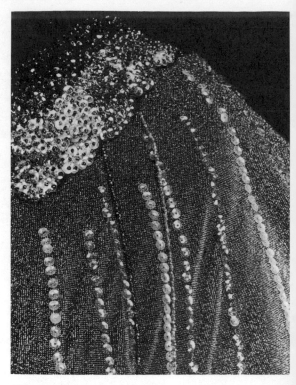

Fig. 36 Shoulder detail of an embroidered collar over a Lurex jersey 'cape' dress

adds weight to a garment so exactness in positioning and proportion of this weight is important. Almost all fabrics can be used but naturally the make-up of the fabric will dictate the type and position of the beading used on a garment.

Beading is often more successful if it is placed on a garment so that the body supports it. Bodices, cuffs and sleeves are such areas of support which help to eliminate the 'drag' which weighty beads can cause. It would be disastrous, for instance, to embroider encrusted isolated motifs on a chiffon skirt as the hemline would dip unevenly. Also the gentle flowing nature of the fabric would be destroyed.

Fine fabrics can be backed to increase their strength and stability providing that the backing does not interfere with the appearance and design of the garment. Net and fine organdie are materials which are most suitable for reinforcing both transparent and fine opaque cloth; however, they

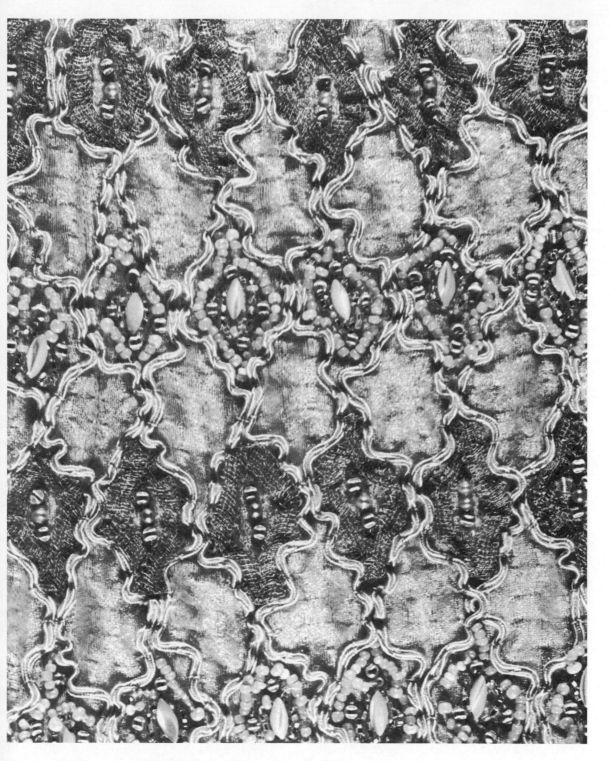

Fig. 37 Portion of a wedding dress bodice, with
Russian braid, ribbon, pearls, buttons and beads,
showing how seams can be concealed

33

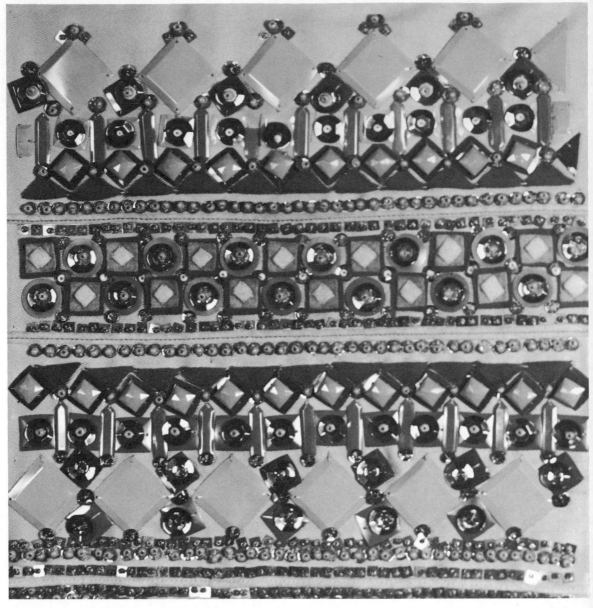

Fig. 38 Border design using felt, square beads, sequins and paillettes

should only be used when they do not interfere with the natural qualities of a fabric. For instance it would be unwise to affect the flowing lines of crêpe with a backing unless the embroidery was put into the supported areas of a garment, where fabric would be naturally fitted to the body.

There are many approaches which can be taken when designing with beads as each different type of bead offers a different design possibility when related to fabric.

1   Each bead can be considered as a single unit and used accordingly.

2   Solid patterns can be built up of one or more types of bead.

3   A single-coloured texture and pattern can be formed using matt and shiny beads.

34

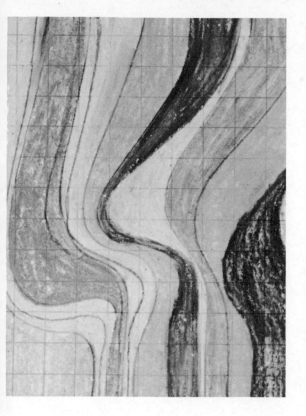

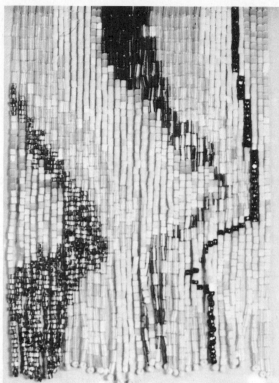

Fig. 39 Beaded fringe with design idea

4 Texture formed by coloured beads can be used to enrich a printed fabric in either an all-over texture or on motifs related to the print.

5 Linear texture can be used to outline printed shapes.

6 Transparent beads and sequins can be used to cover a colourful print and thus transform the surface character and colour of the fabric.

7 Bead fringes, both patterned and plain, can be used to emphasize shape and exaggerate movement (see Fig. 39).

When attaching beads to fabric it is important to use a bead needle and strong fine thread, not so strong that it tears the background fabric with the weight of the beads or so fine that it is easily broken. Fine thread should be waxed by drawing it through a beeswax disc to strengthen it and protect it against rough edges of glass and metal beads. The thread should relate in character to the fabric and, depending on the intended effect, a matching or opposing colour of thread can be used. Interesting, subtle colour changes can be discovered by sewing transparent glass beads on to fabric with varying coloured threads. It is by experiment with different methods of attaching beads that design ideas are stimulated and brought to life.

WAYS OF ATTACHING BEADS

1 One by one as in seeding stitch.

2 Hangers: bring the thread out of the fabric and feed on several beads, take the thread back into the fabric thus forming a loop. It is advisable to limit the length of each loop as tangles may occur whilst working and in wearing the garment.

3 A line of beads on cotton, with one end fixed to the fabric, can be couched into position, the beads being distributed as required.

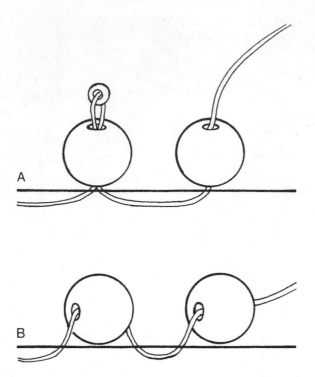

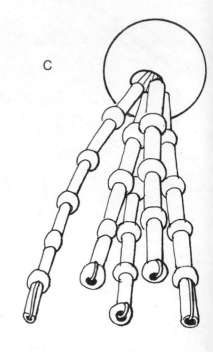

Fig. 40 A, B and C: Ways of attaching beads

4   Beads can be attached singly or severally in a standing position. A combination of standing and flat beads will achieve variety of tone and texture in a design (see Figs. 37, 38 and 44).

5   Pendants are formed like standing beads but longer lengths of smaller beads are used. These simply hang with no tension to hold them erect.

6   Tambour beading is a quick and practical way of attaching beads. All the means of attaching beads described above, with the exception of pendants and standing beads, can be carried out using a frame and tambour hook. The fabric is stretched in or on a frame and the beads are strung out on a continuous thread and attached to the fabric by means of a chain stitch produced by a tambour hook. This is an instrument which resembles a very fine crochet hook. The chain is produced on the wrong side of the fabric, which is uppermost in the frame, while the beads are attached on the underneath of the frame. It is only by practice that any speed in attaching beads is achieved.

SEQUINS

Sequins, like beads, can be bought commercially, but more exciting and personal ones can be punched out of acetate sheeting, felt, PVC, leather and plastic with a leather or pattern punch. These can be attached by the tambour method but more exciting ways of attaching them, combined with beads, can be done by hand sewing.

1   Using a back stitch to produce lines of overlapping sequins (see Fig. 41A).

2   Using a back stitch laying them side by side (see Fig. 41B).

3   Using radial stitches (see Fig. 41C and D).

4   Using double chain stitch as for shisha glass, so that individual sequins or discs are framed and secured (see Fig. 42 A and B).

5   Pendants can be formed, as with beads, but a small bead should terminate them. These can consist of a mixture of sequins and beads.

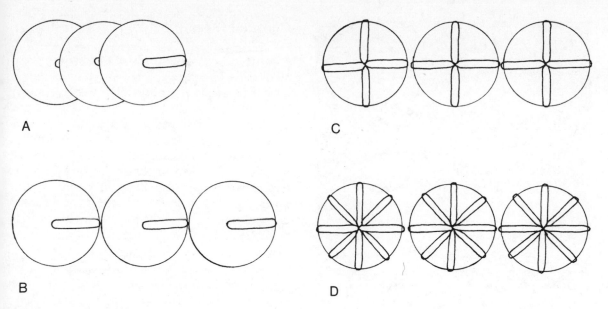

A

C

B

D

Fig. 41 A, B, C and D: Ways of attaching sequins

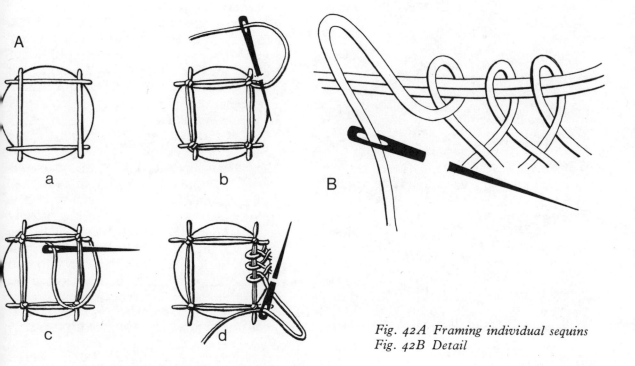

A

a

b

c

d

B

Fig. 42A Framing individual sequins
Fig. 42B Detail

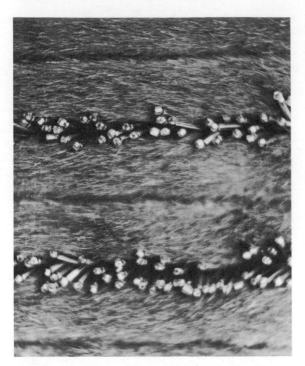

Fig. 43 Pendant beads applied in machined stitch on fur fabric

Fig. 44 Pendants using cinemoid discs and beads

Counted thread

Counted thread methods of embroidery are all of peasant origin and are much in evidence in the national costumes of most European countries.

There are a number of specific types of embroidery which can be included in this group; drawn thread, pulled fabric, needle weaving and net darning (see Fig. 46) to name but a few. All have in common the need for counting the threads of the fabric chosen and each of these methods can, if necessary, be used to achieve a decorated practical and washable garment.

Counted thread work gains much of its appeal from the change it makes to the surface of the fabric. The number and variations of counted thread work methods which are available are extra assets to this kind of work and greatly add to its attraction.

Designing is closely linked with the characteristics of the method and hence is derived the choice of material. Evenness and consistency of weave is important, although in some cases a slub on one of the threads can add interest to a material without seriously affecting these qualities. Ready separation of a fabric's threads is, of course, essential as this characteristic makes easy the drawing out and pulling together of threads (see Fig. 4). It is essential that the individual threads are easily discernible for accuracy in counting which greatly assists the forming of patterns.

Linen, cotton, wool, heavy silk, coarse muslin or voile, or any fabric which has an even weight of both the warp and weft threads, is suitable for counted thread work.

Threads must be strong and not subject to fluffing or wear when being worked. Ideally the stitching threads should match the weight of the fabric threads and for this reason frayed threads, which are removed from the actual fabric to be worked, can be used. Originally these types of embroidery were worked in self-colour on natural linen or cottons. It is self-evident that brightly coloured cloths and threads will bring about

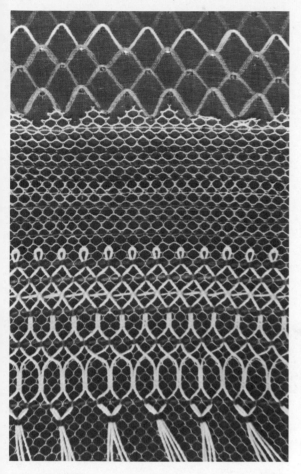

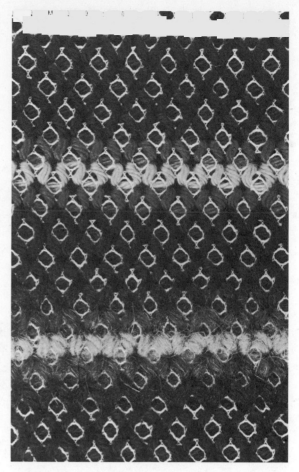

Fig. 45 Net darning and shadow work

Fig. 46 Net darning on cotton net worked in wools

an appearance of gaiety and examples of the effective use of coloured threads on natural or white cloth can be seen in the national costumes of Hungary and Romania.

There is a variety of stitches which can be used to produce differing effects and these would be better dealt with when discussing the different types of counted thread work. Some stitches are common to most while others are peculiar to one.

To produce garments with counted thread decorations it is necessary to try out the stitches and their effects on a separate piece of material. This preparation not only allows practice in technique, but also enables the visual effect which the stitches create to

be seen, so that designs suitable for the embroidery's characteristics can be assessed.

Counted thread embroidery can only be worked in straight lines on either the warp or the weft or in rectilinear shapes, because the very nature of the working method makes it impossible to achieve smooth curves. Curved lines have to be achieved by a series of closely spaced angles.

Like most forms of dress embroidery it is advisable wherever possible to stretch the material in a frame. It can then be loosened in or on the frame to facilitate the working of some of the stitches. Keeping the work taut is particularly necessary when using some man-made fabrics.

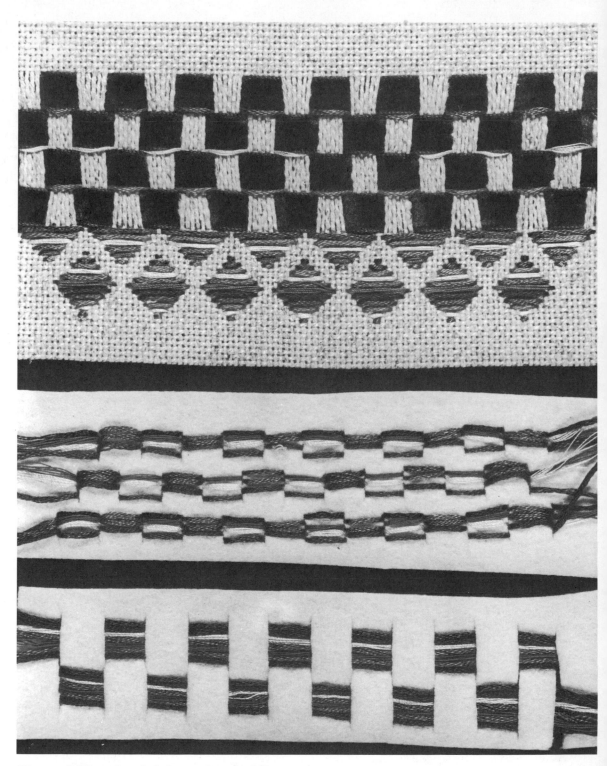

*Fig. 47 Ribbon-threaded drawn thread with
darning showing the progression of the idea
using felt and threads*

Fig. 48A Drawn thread with ribbons

Fig. 48B Detail

DRAWN THREAD WORK

Drawn thread work and needle weaving are very closely allied, each being a treatment of materials which have had selected areas of thread withdrawn. Needle weaving is treated by some as being a separate method altogether but for the purpose of 'fashion embroidery' it is just another form of drawn thread work which tends to produce a heavier, more stable 'woven' type of finish. 'Openwork' or the removal of fabric threads in both directions to leave an empty space, which is then utilized—filled with 'spider's webs' or 'wheels'—provides the most lacy form of decoration.

Excessive use of openwork can weaken the fabric structure; however, the direct effects of this on a finished garment can be minimized by means of mounting it on a lining. The use of a different coloured lining can help to highlight the texture of the embroidery to advantage.

The charm and effectiveness of drawn thread work depends on the removal of certain warp and weft threads and so for fashion embroidery great care has to be taken. The general design to be made out on to the fabric is initially set out into the basic areas

for working, and in so doing care is taken to ensure that no detrimental effect on the hang of the garment will ensue. The detailed design is then worked out on graph paper using the lines to represent the threads of the fabric. If too many threads are removed the fabric is weakened, sagging is the result and the garment will not stand up to wear, especially if no lining is envisaged.

The removal of thread in an isolated motif presents the practical problem of finishing the edges to prevent fraying. Each thread that is withdrawn should have a tail about 76 mm/3 in. left at the edge of the design. These ends can then be woven back into the fabric to produce a non-fraying finished edge (see Fig. 49). Often these areas of weaving can be incorporated into the design, as they give an added tonal effect.

Border designs can be built up by the removal of threads in one direction. Wider borders can be formed by means of increasing the numbers of bands of drawn threads which are separated by strips of intact fabric (see Fig. 48A and B).

Any instability which may result from the removal of these bands of threads can be remedied by the stiffening and hard-wearing

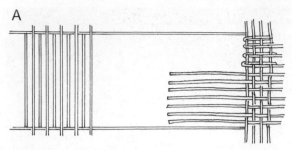

A

Fig. 49A Weaving back ends
Fig. 49B Needle weaving stitch

B

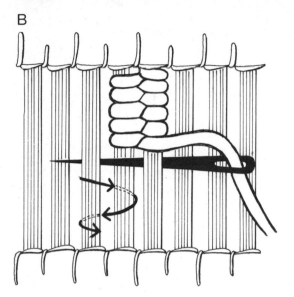

qualities of needle weaving which allows the complete coverage of the remaining threads and thus enables several borders of this kind to be carried out. The embroidery thread is woven around and through the remaining threads in a series of bars, making use of only one basic weaving stitch (see Fig. 49B).

This may sound a little monotonous but the effectiveness of the technique lies in its simplicity and its practicability.

PULLED FABRIC

This method is also called drawn fabric but as this can be confused with drawn thread work the term pulled fabric is more commonly used. The decorative effect of this method is produced by the pulling together of threads or groups of threads and for this reason the term is perhaps more explicit.

As a form of embroidery it is closely allied to needlepoint lace which is of peasant origin, but in the later 'lace' stage it can be attributed to Flanders and Germany. During the eighteenth and early nineteenth centuries it was very popular in England and was used on selected parts of garments such as the fichu collars forming the *décolleté* necklines of the period. The designs used were based on flower and leaf motifs carried out in suitable stitchery with pulled fabric fillers, and worked on such fabrics as cotton and fine muslin.

The popularity of this method revived in the late 1930s and early 1940s but at the time it was generally worked on fine crêpe in self-colour.

Pulled fabric depends on the use of various stitches as a means for changing the texture of the original fabric. These stitches are not meant to be seen since their sole purpose is to pull the warp and weft threads into patterns. However, it is possible to add interest by using different weight threads to produce effects on garments. It must be remembered that too thick a thread will distort or completely hide the threads of the background fabric.

The same criteria of design relating to the even-weave, ease of separability of the threads and accuracy of counting apply to pulled fabric work as they do to all counted thread work.

Pulled fabric, depending on the stitch, can give a lacy appearance to a material without weakening it as much as can drawn thread work. It is this characteristic which makes it an extremely practical embroidery method for use on a garment.

The complete garment or selected areas of it can be worked in all-over backgrounds of drawn fabric, particularly for jacket and dress ensembles where surface contrast of the mix-and-match type could be very effective.

The choice of stitch for an overall background should be bold and simple and not so small in scale that it becomes ineffectual. The simpler the cut of the garment the

Fig. 50 Pulled fabric showing use of 'grafting'
and various thicknesses of thread

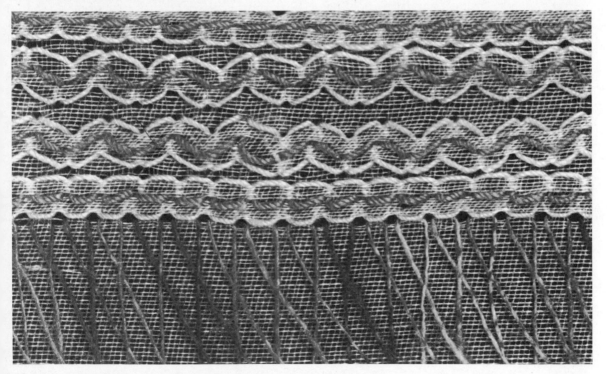

Fig. 51 Pulled fabric on voile with shadow
work

better; the pattern will tend to become distorted by too many seams and the total effect will be lost.

Each individual stitch forms its own directional pattern, being vertical, horizontal or diagonal, and advantage of these geometric pattern possibilities should be taken while planning a garment. Here again ideas can be worked out on graph paper and all-over effects achieved by planning chequered patterns allowing the background fabric and patterned squares to balance in proportion. Borders can be formed from such arrangements and these are best located on bodice portions, skirt hems and sleeves.

Execution of drawn fabric usually necessitates stretching on a frame to ensure that the grain of the material is straight and, in the traditional manner, that the fabric is slightly taut. The small amount of slack which is thus available is essential if the pulling is to be effective. Variation of the stitch tension, from slack through medium to tight, will produce differing surfaces which can lend pulled fabric much of its attraction in a contemporary adaptation of a subtle and delicate technique.

Quilting

Quilting is one of the oldest world-wide forms of embroidery. There is a long-standing tradition of quilting in the British Isles, particularly in the north east around Durham and in south Wales, which has evolved separately, so much so that it has become a native art. The word 'quilt' comes from the Latin *culcita* meaning a stuffed cushion, and quilted garments, formed by the sewing together of various layers of cloth, originated as a means of achieving the functional purposes of both warmth and protection. Roman and mediaeval soldiers wore quilted garments under their armour and chainmail to prevent chafing of the skin.

Garments which were originally purely functional gradually evolved and developed a more decorative form of quilting, the thick padding giving an attractive relief effect. During the eighteenth century quilting was highly favoured, reaching its peak of popularity in the reign of Queen Anne. Petticoats were richly embroidered and quilted, with visual evidence of them peeping through split overskirts. Patterned materials were often used, adding further to the decorative quality of the fabric. More recently, advantage has been taken of the insulating value of quilting and it has been widely employed for outer or over garments.

There are three main types of quilting—English, Italian and Trapunto—each of which possesses its own characteristics and working methods, but the factor which all have in common is surface relief.

All types of quilting can be carried out either by machine stitching or by hand stitching with certain obvious but basic differences in their application. When using a machine it is advisable to use a fairly large stitch and to release the pressure on the machine foot slightly for ease of work and to prevent drag on the material. Hand quilting should be worked on a stretcher in running or back stitch. The needle should enter the fabric perpendicularly so that the stitches are of equal size on the back and the front of the work.

In the past, quilting designs have generally been worked with self-coloured threads, but naturally the size and colour of thread can be varied as long as both needle and thread pass through the fabric and padding easily.

The launderability of a quilted garment depends on the careful selection of washable materials for the constituent parts which make up the selected method of quilting. These parts may include a maximum of three layers, the top fabric, the filling and the lining.

The choice of top fabric depends also on how practical the finished garment has to be. All fabrics except taffeta (which splits) can be used, and sewing threads should correspond with the material, for example,

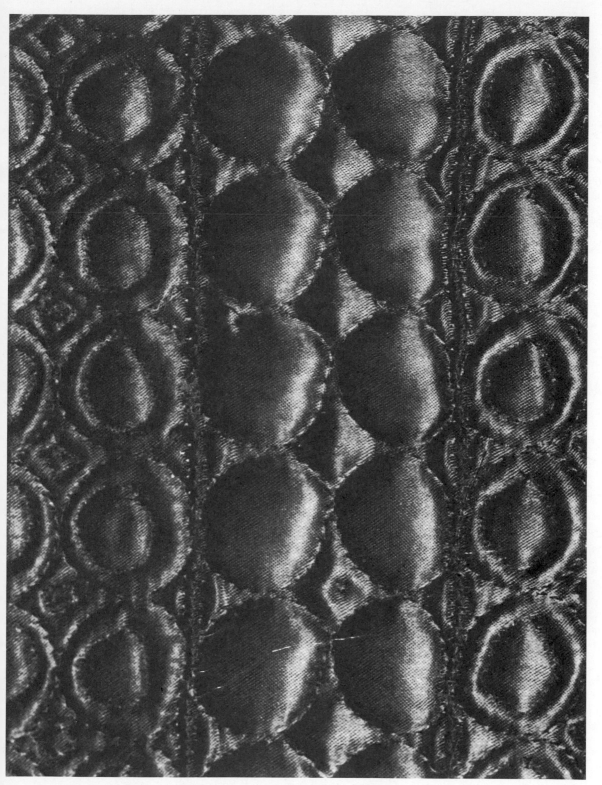

Fig. 52 English quilting on black satin

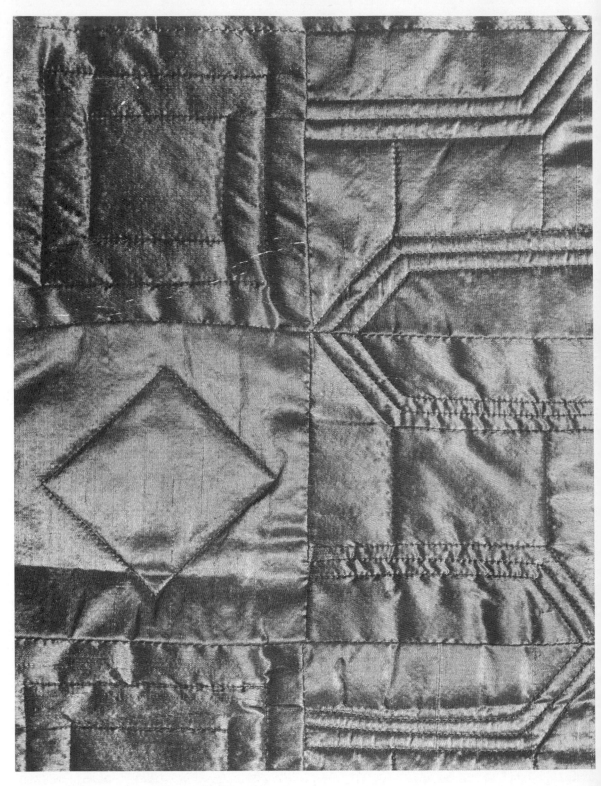

Fig. 53 Portion of a quilted patchwork skirt

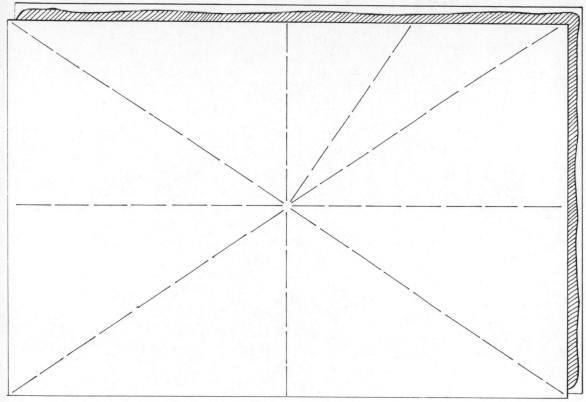

Fig. 54A Tacking out layers of cloth for quilting: radiating from the centre

mercerized thread with silk or satin, and cotton thread with cotton.

Transparent top fabrics can be used to achieve 'shadow quilting' using the Trapunto and Italian quilting methods. Ingenious use can be made of the transparent 'bubbles' and tramlines so formed to trap beads, sequins and brightly coloured wools. A product of this latter method could not, of course, be easily laundered.

Special attention must be given to the suitability of filling material, which may consist of the following: (a) sheep or lambswool, which should be grease free and carded; (b) domette—a loosely knitted fabric with a brushed fluffy surface; (c) Terylene wadding —light in weight and most suitable for dress embroidery.

The lining or backing fabric should be fine in quality to prevent any extra bulk and muslin or lawn and lining silk are eminently suitable materials.

DESIGN

When considering a quilted garment there are many design aspects to take into account before the shape of the garment is decided upon. Initially it must be understood that quilting is essentially a padded, raised surface formed by stitch-line depressions. This undulating surface produces tonal ranges which have to be considered as an element of the garment design and in conjunction with the scale of the quilted pattern relative to the body size.

Secondly, the richness of quilting and the possibility of its being used as an all-over decoration means that the garment would in

B

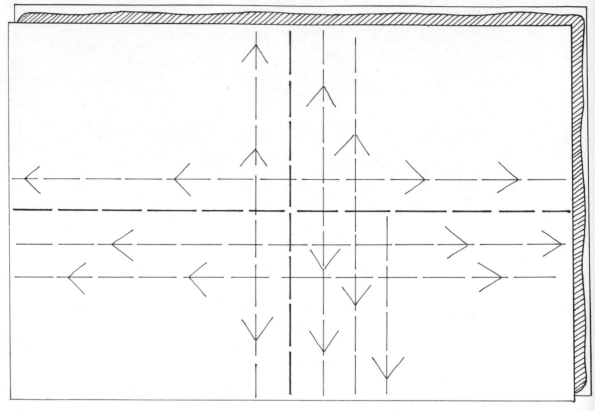

Fig. 54B   Tacking horizontally and vertically

most cases want to be simple in cut, allowing the embroidery to give major impact.

A third point to consider when quilting a garment is the added weight. Only the lightest filling must be chosen to alleviate drag and distortion of the figure shape, particularly at waist, hip and bust areas.

ENGLISH QUILTING

This is the method of quilting which combines a useful function with decoration. The whole area is padded and the design stitched through three layers of material, therefore an overall pattern is the most suitable type of design. Geometric shapes and linear patterns are suitable for producing designs although the traditional template shapes like the scale, shell, feather, elipse and cable can offer exciting pattern possibilities.

If the design is built up from straight lines it can be worked on the machine set for ordinary stitching, but any intricate pattern of curves and circular forms is best stitched as for machine embroidery. Hand stitchery is suitable for any design but should be worked on a frame or stretcher.

The pattern pieces and the quilting design are suitably marked out on to the fabric before the three layers are tacked together. One or more pattern pieces should be marked on the material and adequate seam allowance left between each piece, with additional allowance for shrinkage which will occur after quilting.

The tacking together of the three layers is the next stage; this is an essential process for English quilting and should be done regardless of whether a hand or machine process has been chosen.

Pin the fabric, interlining and backing together and start tacking from the centre and smooth out towards the edges as illustrated (see Fig. 54A and B) until the area is covered. Once the layers have been tacked together the quilting pattern is sewn on by machine or hand. When the quilting is complete it may prove to be necessary for the whole to be damp stretched. The pattern pieces are then checked for size, cut out and made up in the usual way. To avoid bulk at seam allowances the padding can be pared away.

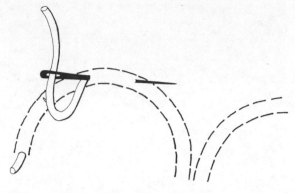

Fig. 55 Italian quilting method

ITALIAN QUILTING

This type of quilting, like Trapunto, differs from English quilting in that it is worked on two layers of fabric, a ground fabric and a backing fabric. Italian quilting is sometimes referred to as cording; the raised effect is achieved by running a cord of fleece or a thread through the parallel lines of stitching which form the design.

The cord of fleece is inserted through the backing fabric using a blunt needle. Where the design lines are curved or at an acute angle the needle is brought out and re-inserted into the same hole and threading is continued. This cord must be left loose to form a loop at this point. The loop prevents tension forming at sharp bends.

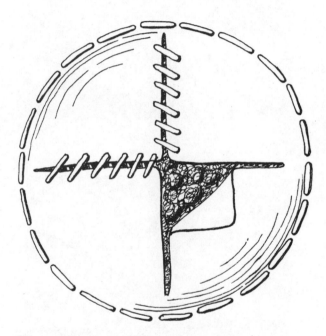

Fig. 56 Trapunto filling and oversewing

TRAPUNTO QUILTING

This, like Italian quilting, is a form of quilting where only certain isolated areas are raised. These can be of any shape though it is advisable to limit the size to achieve evenly padded areas. The contained 'island' motifs which identify Trapunto quilting are padded from the back and the high-relief pattern thus formed is purely decorative. It is because of this quality that Trapunto can be easily combined with other embroidery techniques and quilting types to form contrasts between the solid masses of Trapunto and the line of English and Italian quilting.

Fig. 57 *Detail of quilted jacket with machine-textured area*

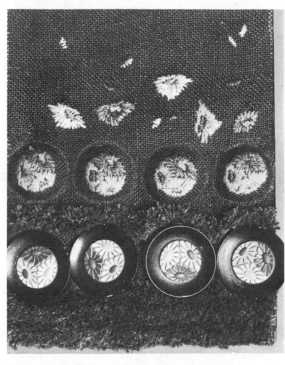

Fig. 58 *A border design using Trapunto quilting, buttons, tufting and hand stitching*

Smocking

The term 'smocking' has arisen from the decorative stitching which was developed to secure gathers of cloth in the familiar shift or smock type of garment which field workers wore in the eighteenth and nineteenth centuries in Great Britain.

This type of decoration is to be found in the national costumes of many countries, including Hungary, Romania and Russia, where the gatherings at cuff and neck edges are given special decorative attention.

DESIGN

Smocking in its present form is most commonly used on children's garments where it is most decorative and, if launderable materials and threads are used, most practical. It also has the advantage of being elastic and will stretch as a child grows.

All kinds of material are capable of being gathered, but for dress embroidery the thickness of a material is a limiting factor and the bulk which a heavy material can produce if gathered needs to be avoided.

Smocking does not rely on colour for its effect. Should colour be used it ought to be simple. Interesting tonal ranges can be achieved using self-coloured threads on a similar background by varying the scale and proportion of patterns.

Gathers are formed by making a series of regularly worked running stitches in straight lines along the weft of a fabric; the weft spanning from selvedge to selvedge. The general spacing for running stitches seems to be as follows: miss four and pick up two fabric threads—although even spacing of stitch and pick-up threads can be used, as shown in Fig. 61A.

There are five basic smocking stitches: vandyke stitch; chevron stitch; stem stitch; cable stitch and honeycomb stitch, each having its own peculiar appearance (see Fig. 61A–F).

One of the great advantages of this dress embroidery method is its elasticity, which

Fig. 59 Glove leather pin-tucked and smocked

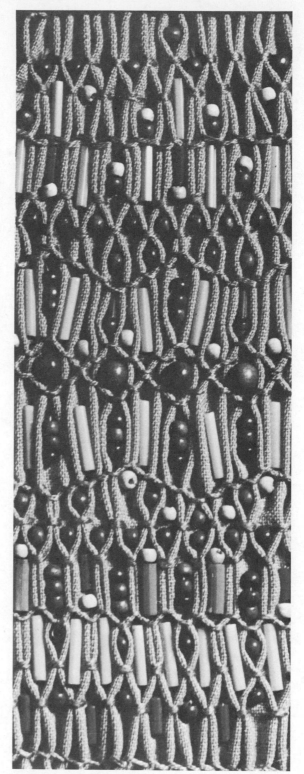

can be varied by means of the stitch and patterns chosen by the worker.

Honeycomb pattern is the most elastic and zig-zag pattern formed by stem stitch the least; thus variations enable the garment to be designed to give firmness and elasticity in the appropriate places.

When preparing for smocking at least three times the actual measurement of cloth is necessary, for example to produce a 203 mm/8-in. panel the amount of fabric required is 609 mm/24 in.

A smocked top should be gathered to a dimension of up to 25 mm/1 in. less than the yoke measurement.

The waist should be gathered to a dimension of up to 77 mm/3 in. less than the waist measurement.

The cuff should be gathered to a dimension of 38 mm/1½ in. less than the wrist measurement.

Before one can evenly gather the cloth together in preparation for smocking some method of providing guide marks for the gathers must be decided upon. This can be

Fig. 60 Beaded smocking

Fig. 61 A Regular gathering stitch
B Vandyke stitch
C Chevron stitch
D Stem stitch
E Cable stitch
F Honeycomb stitch

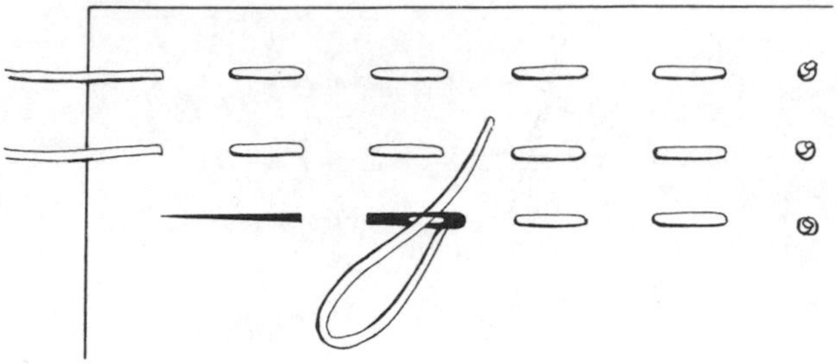

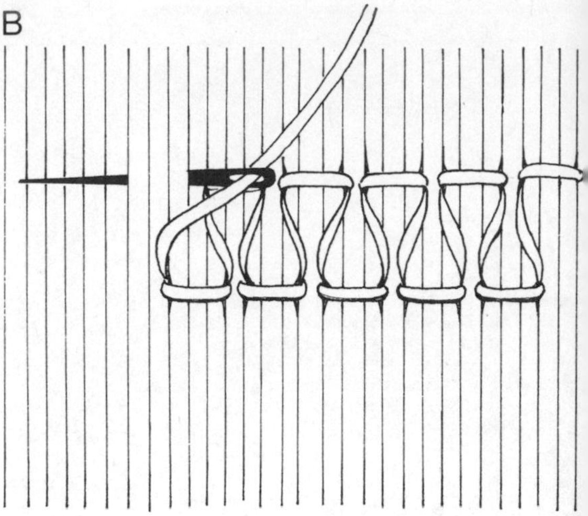

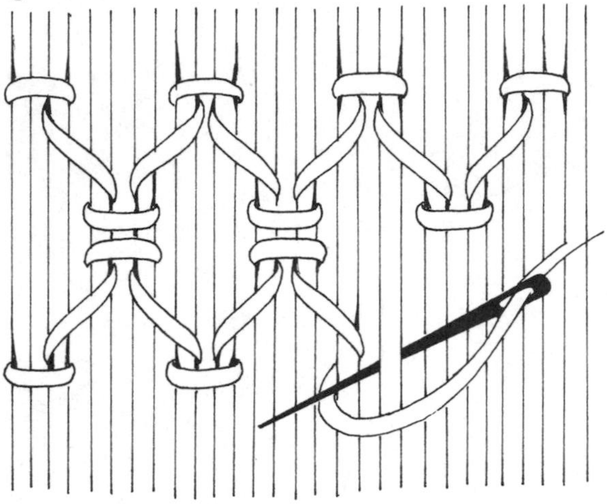

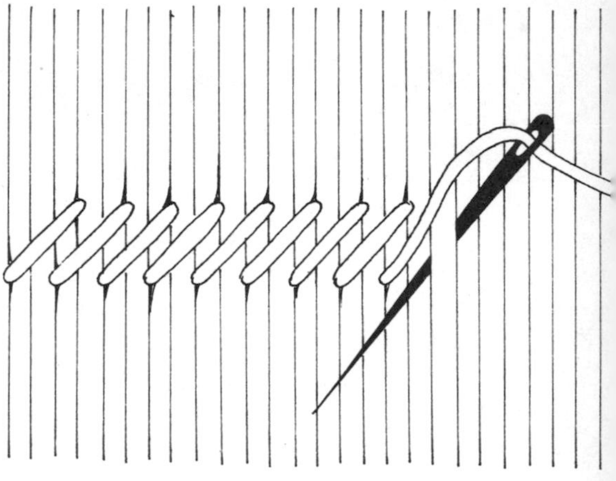

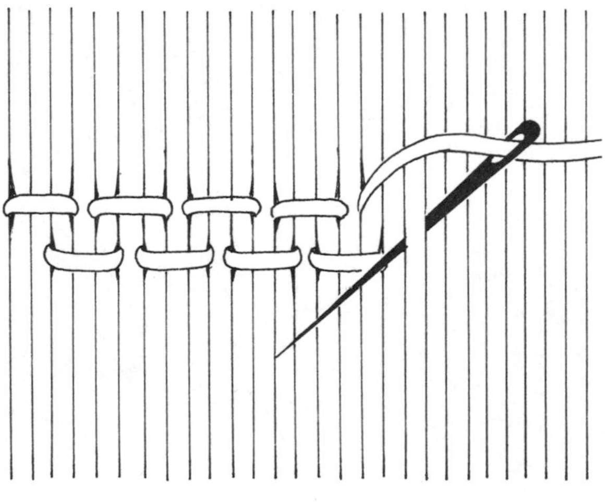

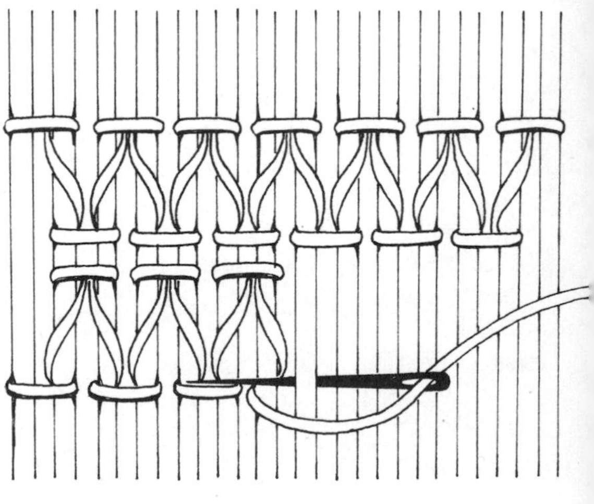

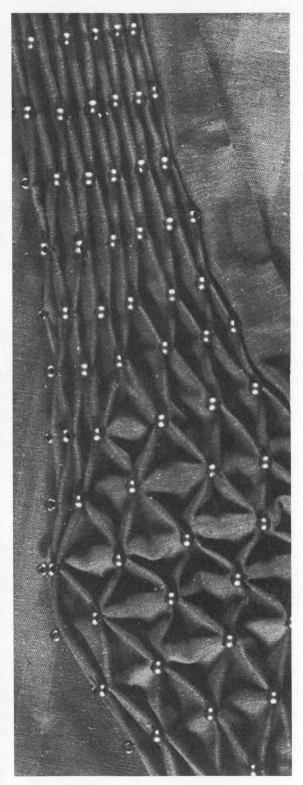

Fig. 62 Beaded honeycomb smocking

selected from one of the following means:

1 Iron dotted transfer paper on to the back of the cloth.

2 Paint dots with poster paint on to the wrong side of the fabric with the aid of a ruler. Pencil spots are sometimes used but graphite does tend to rub off on to fabric, though a hard pencil can be satisfactorily used on an easily launderable fabric like cotton.

3 Count the threads of fabric and gather accordingly.

4 Tack dotted paper firmly on to the fabric, sew through both fabric and paper, remove paper before drawing up the threads into gathers.

5 Make use of even checks, stripes or spots on fabric (see Figs. 62 and 63).

METHOD

Select a gathering thread of a contrasting colour to that of the material. Make a large knot in the thread and, starting from the right-hand side, pick up a small portion of material at each marked position on the wrong side of the work. Unthread the needle on completion of each line and leave the thread lying loose. Complete the required number of rows and then draw up the material into gathers by holding the loose ends of thread in the hand, carefully easing each row along until the desired width for smocking is attained. Secure the loose ends in pairs by twisting around inserted pins.

Work the selected smocking stitches into the even folds on the right side of the work. Choose a thread for the working that is in keeping with the material, for example on linen or similar material use a linen or mercerized thread; for muslin or silk use a twisted embroidery thread. On completion of work the gathering threads are removed.

Where smocking is prepared for a dress it is advisable to smock the area first using the basic measurements given and then lay the pattern pieces down on the smocked and plain fabric. This method requires no damp stretching.

*Fig. 63 Honeycomb smocking on striped cotton
with applied ribbons*

54

7 Machine Embroidery

Machine embroidery has its roots firmly planted in the industrial revolution of the eighteenth century when many differing inventions from various countries formed the basis from which the machine embroidery industry in Britain and the Continent developed and flourished in the 1870s. The earliest invention was in 1778 and it took nearly seventy-five years before the first domestic machine, as opposed to industrial machines, became a practicable proposition.

Work which was produced from these domestic machines was very limited because it was mainly slavish imitation of the traditional methods and designs of hand embroidery. It was not until the 1930s that the creative potential of the embroidery machine was first considered. A Miss M. E. G. Thomas of the Bromley College of Art began experimenting with the free use of the machine, using it as a drawing implement and exploiting the different stitches which were available. There were many advocates of this new approach, of whom Rebecca Crompton was the best known, but the firms who were mass-producing embroidered work objected to the free use of 'their' machines and attempted to obstruct their use by legal means. Ironically, some hand embroidery purists added their support to the industrial firms. The possibilities of the new approach, despite these early set-backs, were quickly comprehended and the 'machine' became accepted as a useful tool for the embroiderer.

Machine embroidery can be divided into two types, the first of which is *free style*, whereby the presser foot and teeth are removed from contact with the cloth and the needle is used as a pencil. The work has to be tightly stretched in an embroidery ring.

The second type is worked with both the foot and teeth in operation. No frame is needed which means that almost any type of machine, whether it is powered by hand or electricity, is suitable for this work. Electric machines are preferred as both hands are left free for controlling the work under the machine.

It is essential that the machine embroiderer should understand the full potential of the machine and be confident enough to change tensions and easily return them to normal sewing conditions. New stitches and textured effects can be produced by experimenting with varying top and bottom tensions combined with differing threads. It is advisable to make special samples and to record the varying tensions which are used in their production. In this way they can easily be reproduced on garments if desired.

FREE EMBROIDERY

Most machines can be used provided the feed or teeth can be put out of action and the presser foot removed so that the fabric in the ring can be passed under the needle in any direction. A lever or knob can usually be found on the machine to release this contact

Fig. 64 Sample showing line and tone variations

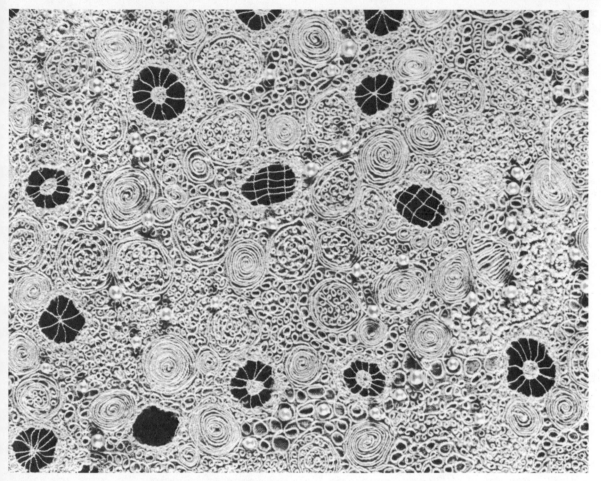

Fig. 65 Detail of organdie bodice using whip stitch, spider's webs and pearls

with the fabric. Some older machines can be fitted with a raised plate to cover the teeth.

The possibilities of this type of decoration are unlimited provided the operator knows the full repertoire of the machine, whether it be a straight stitch machine or of the swing-needle type. The only restriction imposed by this method is the essential use of a ring frame to keep the cloth taut, like a drum, so that it allows a smooth action of the needle and a free-flowing movement of cloth. Vanishing muslin can be used to stiffen the material as this obviates the use of a ring, but it is not always advisable as heat has to be applied to enable it to fall away from the embroidered cloth.

Some fabrics show a ring mark when the ring is removed; this can be avoided by binding the inner ring of the ring frame or by inserting a second layer of fabric between the inner ring and the work.

If the fabric to be embroidered is too small for the ring it can be tacked to a larger piece of fabric on the straight of grain and then placed in the ring. Rings can be bought in several sizes and problems can arise if the ring is too small in comparison with the area to be embroidered. This can be solved by moving the ring along the fabric being embroidered.

When using a ring for free embroidery care must be taken not to over-embroider one area as the build-up will force apart the threads and splitting of the fabric could result.

The following effects result from changes in tension:

Whip stitch

Basic whip stitch is achieved by increasing the top tension and loosening the bottom tension. The latter is done by either slightly loosening the screw on the spool case, as on the more modern machines, or on the fixed spool receptacle on the older machines. The loosened bottom tension causes the bottom thread to whip up over the tight top thread giving the stitch its characteristic appearance. Variations in the amount of whipping are achieved by moving the ring at different speeds while the machine is running fast. Basically the slower the ring is moved the more whipping builds up over the top thread which lies on the surface of the cloth. The right side of the work is uppermost in the ring.

Cable stitch

Threads which are too thick to be threaded through the needle eye can be used in the spool. They must be wound evenly on to the spool by hand. In the case of Lurex or any bobbined thread however, a pencil can be slipped through the spool or bobbin and the pencil held in both hands while the spool empties and feeds on to another spool mechanically wound by the machine. Stranded cotton, perlé thread, wool, buttonhole twist and Anchor soft thread are all suitable for use as the spool thread for this method of stitching. Ordinary machine thread is used on the top of the machine. The spool tension is loosened or removed altogether and the top tension left at normal, or tightened depending on the amount of texture required. A bouclé effect is the result of no bottom tension on the thicker thread and a fairly normal top tension. The fabric is placed in the ring, wrong side uppermost, so that the whole design can be marked on the wrong side and easily followed. The thicker spool thread which forms the texture is thus presented on the lower, right side of the fabric.

The following effects are achieved with normal tension stitching:

Zig-zag and satin stitch

Zig-zag and satin stitch can be used in the same way as the above methods, employing varying colours to achieve textured effects, but perhaps their most interesting use for dress is the pulled fabric effect. This is achieved by machining on open-weave fabrics or on fabrics which have had some threads removed.

Spider's webs

The attractive lacy effect given by the use of 'spider's webs' is more suitable for transparent fabrics but can be used on fine non-fraying cottons and fine wools. Simple geometric designs using a straight machine stitch are most suited to this method. The material is placed in a frame and shapes are drawn on with two parallel lines of straight stitch closely placed together. Zig-zag or satin stitch can be used as an outline but have to be carefully done to achieve an even line. All shapes are first worked in this manner. The piece is then removed from the frame and the inside shapes cut out with a fine pair of scissors. It is advisable just to cut the shapes in the section that is going to be immediately worked on, to avoid stretching of the cut shapes.

This section is then replaced in the frame and lines are machined across the holes, spanning the hole in a spider's web pattern. At intersections of lines a few stitches should be worked over one another to reinforce the junction. The scale of each hole is important for if the hole is too large distortion and drag can occur. With experiment, this limiting factor tends to become obvious.

Fig. 66 Zig-zag on fur fabric

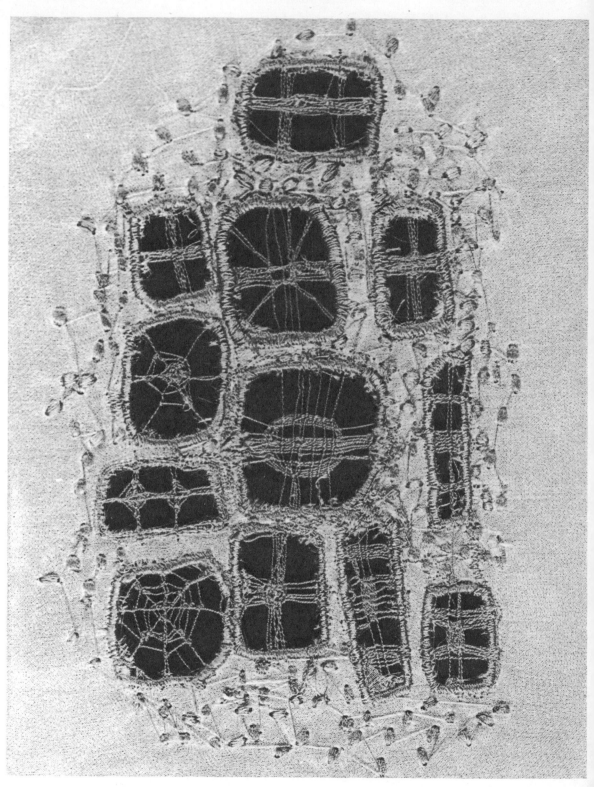

Fig. 67 Spider's webs

Plate 1 Log-cabin patchwork
Plate 2 Curled procion-dyed organdie with
decorative machined edge

Plate 3 Gold rings, beads and braid

Plate 4A Gold Lurex machined on purple

Plate 4B Purple thread machined on brown

WORKING WITH THE PRESSER FOOT AND TEETH IN ACTION

When working in this manner the design will tend to be restricted to straight lines and points as the natural backward and forward action of the machine lends itself to this, but curvilinear shapes can be achieved with a little patience and experience. A great number of surface textures can be formed merely by using the straight stitch or zig-zag stitch to lay down groups of threads on the surface of the cloth. Besides these there are the effects like tucking and cording, hemstitching and tailor tacking (see Figs. 69 and 73), which are produced with the use of special attachments. All these can transform an otherwise rigid way of working into an exciting end-product, particularly if the automatic machine patterns are combined with tucking and double needle lines. The straight stitch, zig-zag and other patterns on these machines tend to appear to be very conventional but when freely combined can come into their own for dress embroidery, particularly for edgings on organdie and for border patterns.

Almost all fabrics, from the heaviest brocade to the finest organza or net, can be used for machine embroidery of both types. The only fabrics which are not suitable are those which stretch, like jersey and crêpe, the reason being that they cannot be stretched in a ring without distorting the warp and the weft threads. It is essential to keep these at right angles or the fall of the finished garment on the body will tend to be permanently askew. A backing fabric can be used to counteract this stretch but by doing so the natural property of the fabric is lost. The decision not to use a backing fabric with stretch material does depend on the positioning of the embroidery on the garment, for instance, the stitching may form a band or belt which need not affect the fall of the garment.

Although this chapter deals mainly with the use of the domestic machine, mention of the now common industrial machines may prove to be helpful.

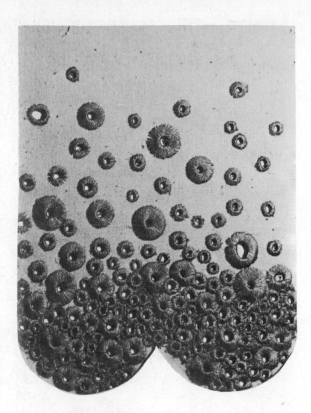

Fig. 68 Eyelet edging

The Irish machine, Cornelly machine and the Tufter machine are the most commonly used. The Irish machine does running stitch and zig-zag and is solely designed for machine embroidery. It has no presser foot, bar or teeth and therefore necessitates the use of an embroidery ring. The biggest advantage of this machine is that it can make up to 13 mm/½-in. wide zig-zag or satin stitch, the increase in width from straight stitch is controlled by means of a knee press which leaves the hands free. Varying widths of stitching can be controlled manually by changing the knee pressure, and even-width stitches by means of locking the control to a preselected size.

The Cornelly machine is basically for producing chain stitching, the size of which can be varied. With attachments the machine can be used for braiding. By turning the hook on the needle so that it faces the back of the machine and adjusting the driving

Fig. 69 Tailor tacking lines with flowers

Fig. 70 Cornelly cording on knitted fabric

worm under the machine a mossing texture can be produced.

The Tufter, as the name suggests, produces tufts like candlewick which can be sheared to produce light and shade (see Fig. 58). This effect is similar to that produced by the tailor's tack foot attachment supplied with some domestic machine kits. Neither of the two latter machines requires the use of an embroidery ring.

8 Manipulating Fabrics

Throughout the book the potential of varying embroidery techniques as related to fabric has been investigated, but little or nothing has been said about the manipulative qualities of fabrics. Manipulation has no easily definable history but overlapping with traditional techniques such as smocking does occur.

The term 'manipulation' means to arrange dextrously, deal skilfully with, and here it is related directly to the skilful and ingenious handling of a fabric in the context of integral decoration; that is: using only the material required to form the garment. It thus omits the link between 'embroidery' and fabric which implies an alien or added decoration.

The creation of a wearable, practical garment which incorporates manipulated material as its means of decoration, involves the maker in a great deal of experimental ground-work prior to having thoughts about the garment design, to obtain as many tonal variations and pattern relationships as possible from a given material.

At this simple stage there is a danger of over complicating the ideas which the many possibilities of each material present. A decision has to be made which will define and simplify the approach to the design potential of each method.

Is the fabric to remain whole?
Is the fabric to be destroyed in some way?
Is the fabric to be destroyed and reconstructed?

These are some of the questions which must be asked, because in answering them in relation to the many techniques available (of which tucking, gathering, pleating, interlacing and strap work are but a few), it becomes obvious that a single choice has to be made. Confusing and perhaps conflicting mixtures of techniques can thus be avoided.

It is only after the practical experience gained in investigating one or more of these ideas that the design of a garment incorporating a particular method should be embarked upon. The method thus selected will generally predetermine the basic design limitations of the garment.

It is useful to consider the simple design idea involving the introduction of decoration to break up a garment into contrasting areas of plain and decorated fabrics. Bold use can be made of the contrast formed between the manipulated and non-manipulated fabric and the exciting relationships which result from these contrasts will assist considerably in producing a desirable and sophisticated garment.

Tucking

Opportunity for achieving surface change by means of tucking is manifold as it is related to folding, gathering and pleating. Each of these can be directionally constructed with all variations between horizontal and vertical, depending on the decorative and functional requirements of the method chosen.

Fig. 71 Tonal variations formed by folding material

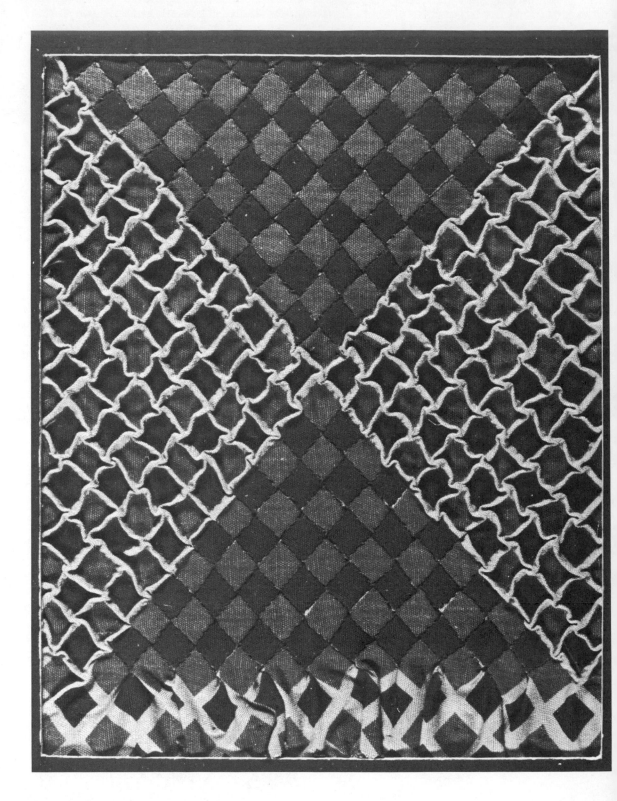

Fig. 72 Tucked diamond-printed material

Fig. 73 Tucking with braid, beads and flowers

The effectiveness of folding and tucking printed fabric can be demonstrated by the striking changes in the character of a print, not only in its surface texture but also in colour. More intense pattern areas can be produced by cleverly tucking out the ground colour and, because of their rectilinear nature, spotted, checked or striped fabrics are the most successful. The materials used in this way, of necessity, tend to bulk together.

Excessive bulk must be avoided, of course, and should it occur it can be remedied by cutting back the fabric after securing the folds with hand or machine stitchery.

Purely decorative tucking is most suitable for inset areas on a garment, whereas purely functional vertical tucking and pleating which controls the fullness of the fabric relative to the human form becomes a major design feature of the garment.

Fig. 74 Suède folded with knitted insets

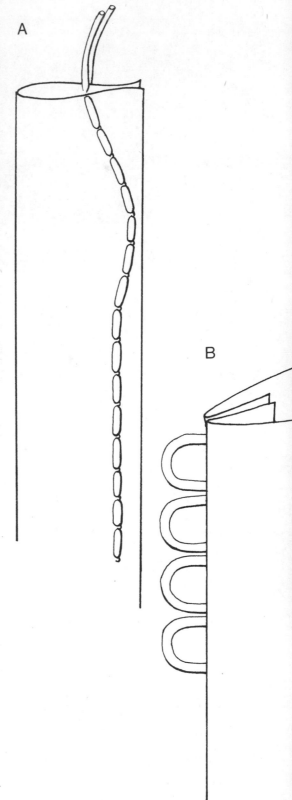

Rouleaux

Rouleaux are formed by cutting 9 mm/$\frac{3}{8}$-in. wide strips of fabric with the grain on the true cross, folding right sides together, stitching along one edge and using the technique illustrated to turn the 'pipe' inside out (see Fig. 75A). Fine piping cord or thick knitting wool can be used inside the 'pipe' to strengthen it. This rouleau can then be used to form the traditional rouleau loops which are used as a replacement for buttonholes. Rouleau loops of this kind can act as a base to interlace other rouleaux (see Fig. 75B), thus extending a traditional method of manipulation.

This idea can be adapted and extended so that the rouleau is used independently; long lengths can be manipulated to form lace-like edgings to garments, insertions, belts and girdles and, with a little ingenuity, fringes. The study of simple knitting and

C

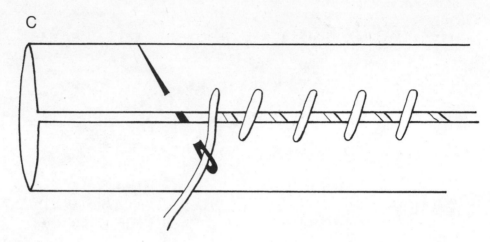

Fig. 75A Making a rouleau
      B Forming a rouleau edge
      C Making a strip
      D Marking out pattern piece on woven strips

D

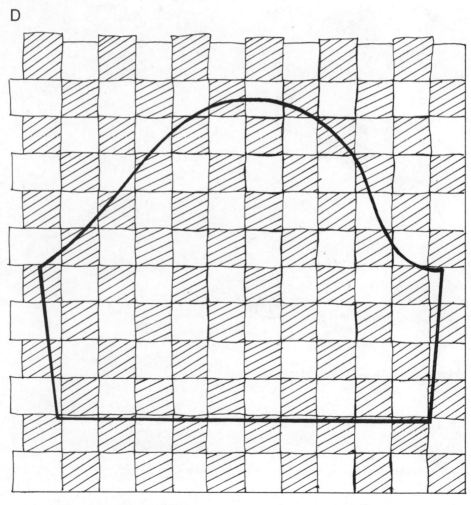

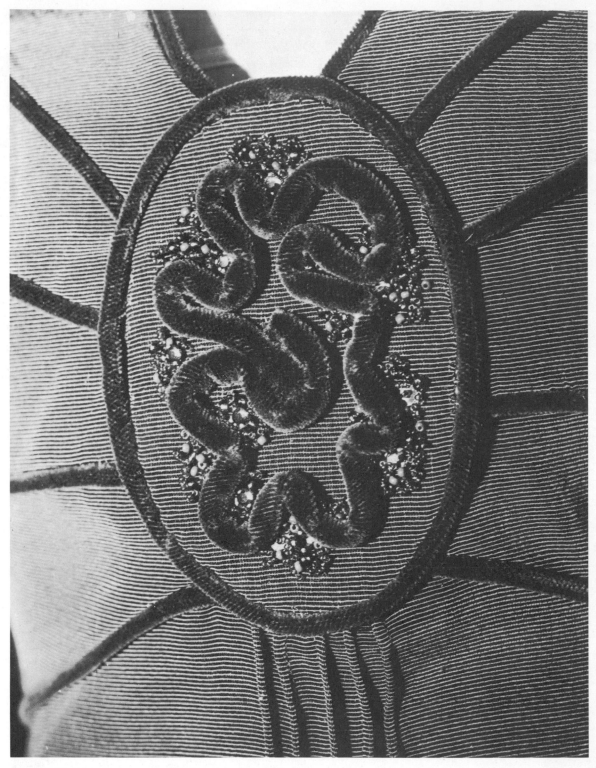

Fig. 76 Stiffened toss on bodice front using
velvet rouleaux and beads

Fig. 77 *Rouleau edging to a jacket*

Fig. 78 *Printed fabric rouleaux with beads on chiffon*

Fig. 79A *Rouleaux on net*

Fig. 79B *Rouleau construction*

Fig. 80A *Woven strips with felt flowers*

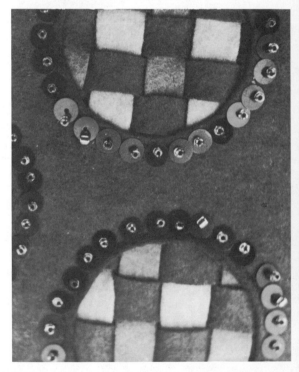

Fig. 81 *Insets of woven felt strips with beads and sequins*

macramé principles can provide stimuli for initiating preliminary working samples; here again simplicity of concept is essential.

The fabric forming the rouleaux must be cut on the true cross so that the rouleaux are easily manipulated to form curves without any wrinkling or buckling. This basic method of making rouleaux and intertwining them bears some similarity to forming strips for basket weaving.

Basket weaving using fabric strips

The fabric is cut into strips, on the straight or the cross, depending on the quality of the fabric. The edges are turned under to meet and sewn together with over-casting stitch to form flat strips (see Fig. 75C). Strips which are to be cut on the cross should be treated with fine iron-on Vilene to prevent the strips from stretching. These strips are then interwoven to form a fabric, the expanding quality of which allows it to mould around the body shape, particularly when the basket weave is used diagonally.

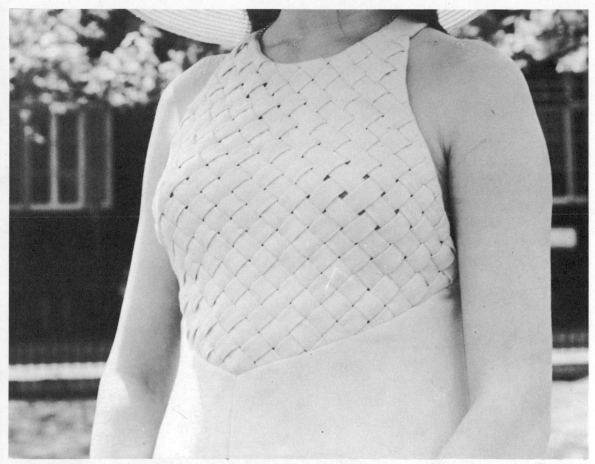

Fig. 80B Diagonally woven strips on a bodice

Fig. 82 French knitting and machine-edged suède strips

73

Fabrics like velvet, which are much too thick to turn under, can have the edges reinforced with machining and the strips thus become a single thickness of velvet. The machined edge is worked prior to cutting the fabric, thus solving the problem of frayed and stretched edges.

If a whole garment area, like a sleeve or bodice, is to be worked in this way, a large enough area must first be woven, then secured by tacking and the pattern piece marked out in the normal way (see Fig. 75D). At this stage, before the pattern piece is cut down, it is advisable to machine stitch a further reinforcing line around the whole pattern piece just a fraction outside the tacked pattern line.

Openwork

As the term implies, openwork consists of an arrangement of openings cut through a material. In appearance this can be rectilinear or lattice-like with certain parts of the fabric 'lattice' having the fabric itself as an infill. It can also be curvilinear with the same principle of holes and infill panels as the basis of design.

Garments making use of openwork are deliberately designed for the effect they produce by virtue of the see-through areas.

The practical problems of executing this work are overcome in the following ways:

The fabric used must be of the non-fraying variety over which the desired

Fig. 83A Felt jacket detail

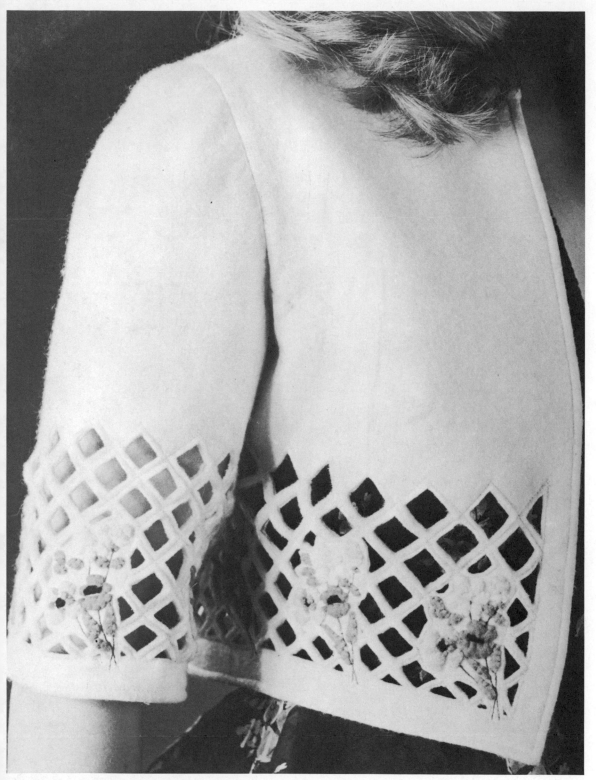

Fig. 83B Felt jacket over printed dress

Fig. 84 Felt cut and rolled

Fig. 85 Felt cut borders

pattern is machined in a single or double line of stitching (depending on how durable it must be), and then the selected portions are wholly or partly cut away between the stitching lines. If the units are only partly cut away they can be rolled or folded to produce a novel surface relief (see Fig. 84).

Openwork garments are not very durable but the interesting and unusual appearance makes them desirable for special occasions.

Plate 5 *Felt openwork with counterchange pattern*

Plate 6 *Folded and cut felt*

Plate 7 *Woven tapes*

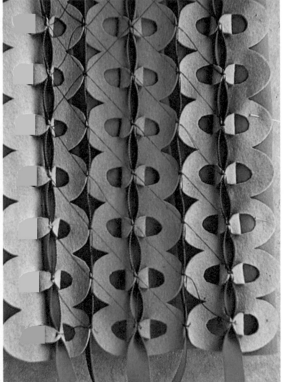

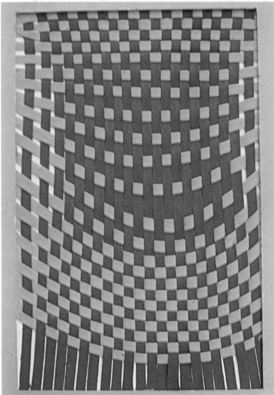

Plate 8 Machine-drawn thread

Plate 9 Bodice layout showing shoulder seams

Worked Examples

Fig. 86A Bodice with transfer-print background decorated with machine embroidery and ribbons

Fig. 86B Detail of bodice

Fig. 87A Sleeve with tie-dye birds on a machine-embroidered background

Fig. 87B Detail of sleeve embroidery

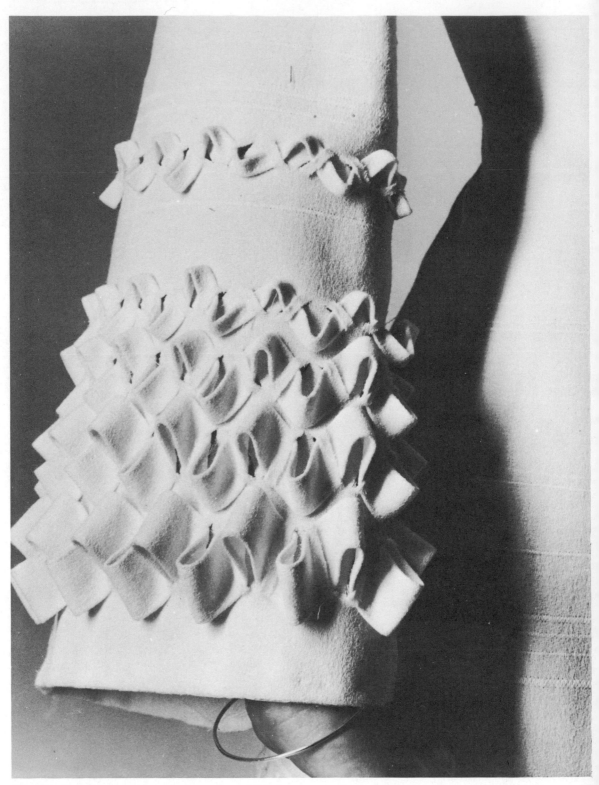

Fig. 88 Detail of a sleeve showing slotted fabric

Fig. 89 Idea for a bikini, using felt and buttons

Fig. 90 Border of folded ribbons

Fig. 91 Detail of a georgette and satin dress with appliqué letters on two layers

Fig. 92 Detail of a bodice decorated with french knots and feathers

Fig. 93 *Machine quilting*

Fig. 94 Machine quilting with free-standing flowers on printed fabric

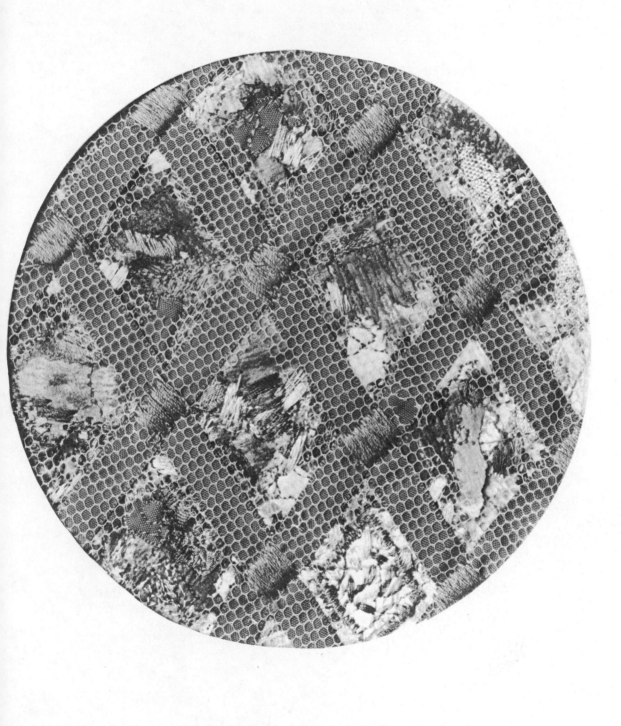

Fig. 95 Ribbon lattice over machine embroidery, masked with net

Fig. 96 Padded fabric flowers

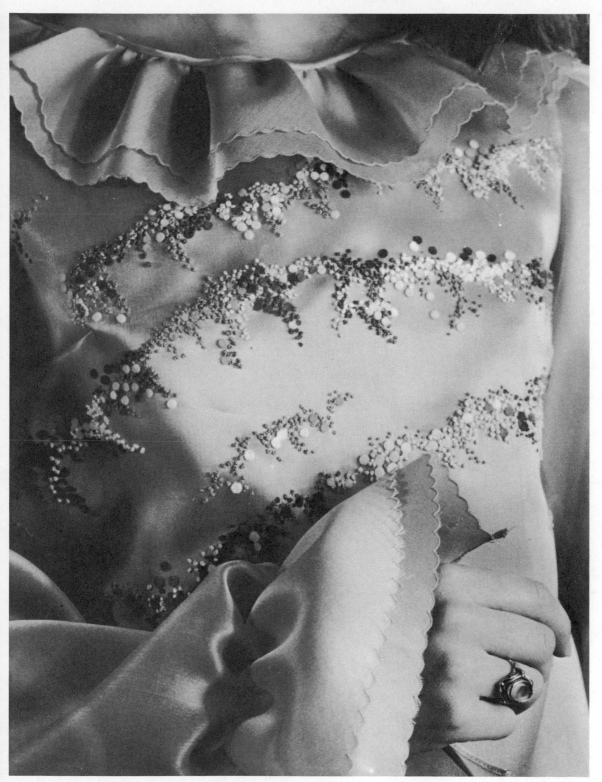

Fig. 97 French knots and felt spots on an organza blouse

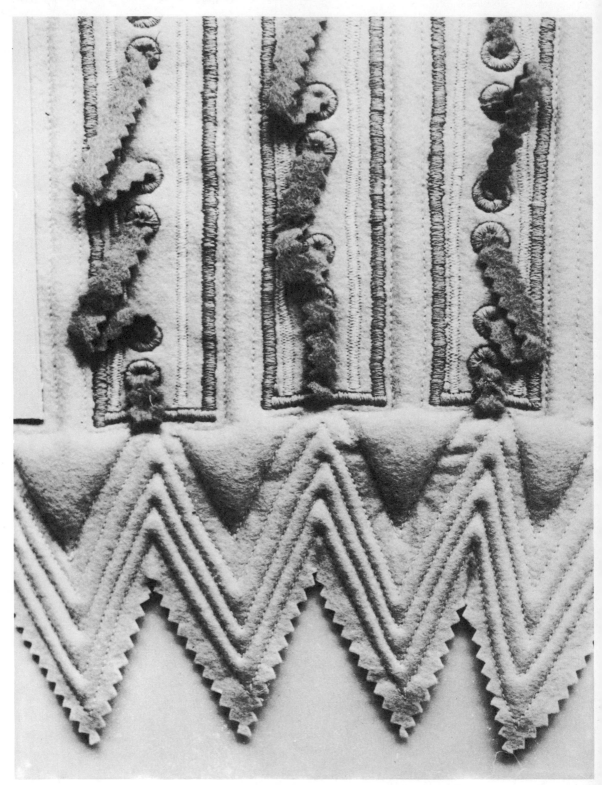

Fig. 98 Italian and Trapunto quilting on pinked felt with threaded eyelet holes

Fig. 99 Rolled felt with sequins

Fig. 100 A beaded border

Fig. 101 Double needle stitching with beads

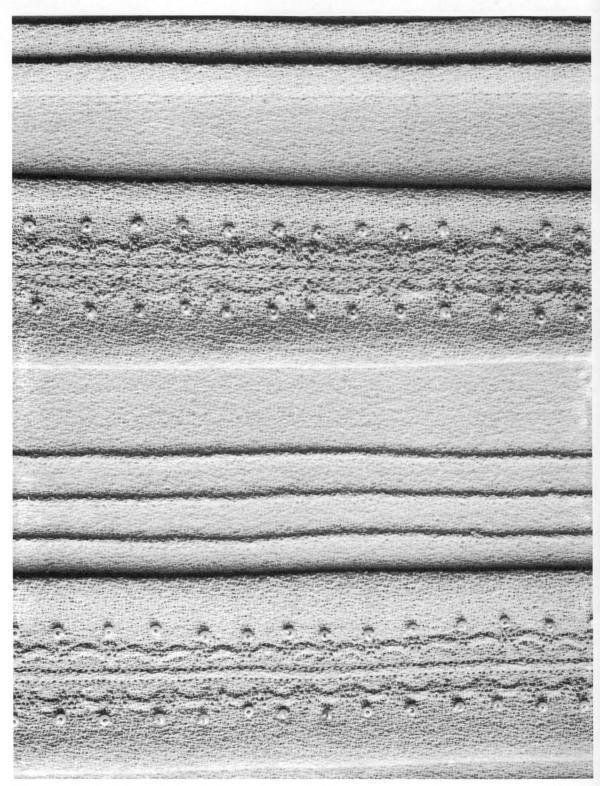

Fig. 102 Wool crêpe, tucked and pleated, decorated with automatic machine embroidery and beads

Fig. 103 Woven strips with applied felt flower shapes

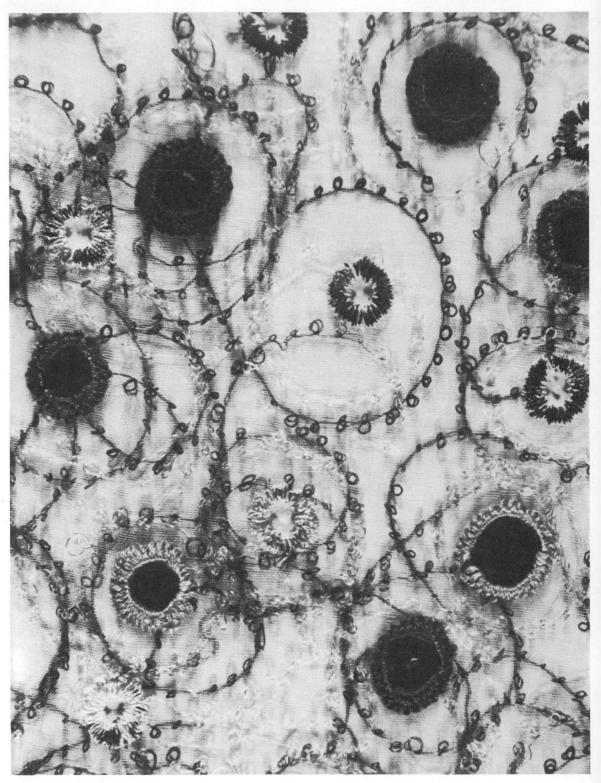

Fig. 104 Machined eyelet holes, shisha glass and Cornelly mossing

Fig. 105 Late Edwardian diamanté decoration with couched silver thread

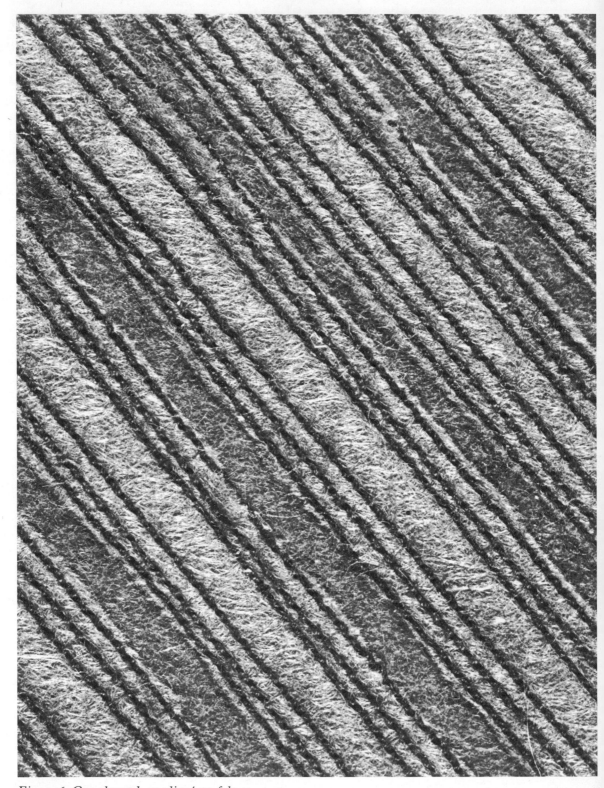

Fig. 106 Cut-through appliqué on felt

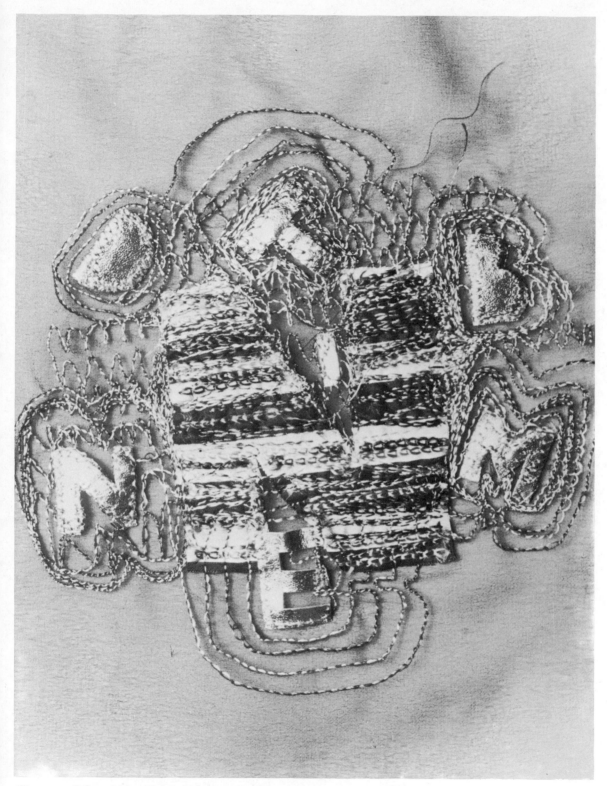

Fig. 107 Silver kid and fabric letters machine embroidered on chiffon

Bibliography

Clucas, Joy, *Your Machine for Embroidery* (George Bell).

Dillmont, Thérèse de, *Encyclopedia of Needlework* (DMC Distrib: Bailey Bros. & Swinfen Ltd).

Edwards, Joan, *Bead Embroidery*.

Hill, M. H. & Bucknell, P. A., *The Evolution of Fashion: Pattern and Cut 1066–1930* (Batsford).

Ickis, M., *The Standard Book of Quilt Making and Collecting* (Dover Publications).

Itten, J., *The Elements of Colour* (Van Nostrand Reinhold).

Laury, J. R., *Quilts and Coverlets: A Contemporary Approach* (Van Nostrand Reinhold).

MacNeil, M., *Pulled Thread* (Mills and Boon).

Mann, Kathleen, *Peasant Costume in Europe* (Black).

Melen, L., *Drawn Thread Work* (Van Nostrand Reinhold).

Munsell, A. H., *A Grammar of Colour* (Van Nostrand Reinhold).

Ostwald, W., *The Colour Primer* (Van Nostrand Reinhold).

Risley, C., *Machine Embroidery* (Studio Vista).

Thomas, M., *Mary Thomas' Embroidery Book* (Hodder & Stoughton).

Thomas, M., *Dictionary of Embroidery Stitches* (Hodder & Stoughton).

Anchor Manual of Needlework, J & P Coats (Batsford).

100 Embroidery Stitches, J & P Coats (Anchor Embroidery).

Index